Hard-Boiled Anxiety

Hard-Boiled Anxiety

The *Freudian Desires* of Dashiell Hammett, Raymond Chandler, Ross Macdonald, and Their Detectives

Karen Huston Karydes

for Jane - Jane Steele,
you are the best work
friend I ever had.
love, Karen - Karen Karydes
March 1, 2016

Hard-Boiled Anxiety: The Freudian Desires of Dashiell Hammett, Raymond Chandler, Ross Macdonald, and Their Detectives

For information about this title, contact the publisher:
Secant Publishing
615 N. Pinehurst Ave.
Salisbury MD 21801
www.secantpublishing.com

 SECANT
PUBLISHING

Library of Congress Control Number: 2014958598
ISBN: 978-0-9909380-6-4

Printed in the United States of America

Cover Design: theBookDesigners
Illustration: Scott Erwert
Interior Design: WESType Publishing Services, Inc.

for Benjamin,
Nathaniel, Alexander,
and Thaddeus

and for Lewis Dabney,
who taught me how to write a book

Permissions

Excerpts

Hammett, Jo. *Dashiell Hammett: A Daughter Remembers* by Jo Hammett. Edited by Richard Layman. New York: Carroll & Graf, 2001. Courtesy of Jo Hammett and Richard Layman.

THE LONG EMBRACE: RAYMOND CHANDLER AND THE WOMAN HE LOVED by Judith Freeman, copyright © 2007 by Judith Freeman. Used by permission of Pantheon Books, an imprint of the Knopf Doubleday Publishing Group, a division of Penguin Random House LLC. All rights reserved.

Reprinted with the permission of Scribner, a Division of Simon & Schuster, Inc., from ROSS MACDONALD: A BIOGRAPHY by Tom Nolan, 1999. All rights reserved.

"The Kenneth Millar Papers." MS-L001. Special Collections and Archives, The UC Irvine Libraries, Irvine, California; and used with the permission of Norman Colavincenzo, Literary Executor of the Estate of Kenneth Millar and Trustee of the Margaret Millar Charitable Trust.

Photographs

Jose Dolan, c. 1915. Courtesy of Josephine Hammett Marshall

Mary and Jo Hammett, c. 1930. Courtesy of Josephine Hammett Marshall

Dashiell Hammett, 1933. Granger, NYC

Lillian Hellman, 1941. Photofest

Cissy Pascal, c. 1913. Raymond Chandler Papers (Collection 638). UCLA Library Special Collections, Charles E. Young Research Library

Raymond Chandler, 1918. Photograph by Mina Whiting. Raymond Chandler Papers (Collection 638), UCLA Library Special Collections, Charles E. Young Research Library

Raymond Chandler, 1939. Photofest

Raymond Chandler, c. 1947. George Platt Lynes/*Condé Nast* Archive/CORBIS

Kenneth Millar, c. 1921. Photographed by Mary V. Carr. Courtesy of Tom Nolan

The Millar Family, 1948. *Kitchener Waterloo Record* Negative Collection, University of Waterloo Library

Ross Macdonald, 1975. Photofest

Eudora Welty, c. 1970s. Photofest

Contents

Introduction   ix

Chapter One   **Sons and Fathers**   1
Chapter Two   **Sons and Mothers**   37
Chapter Three   **Sons and Lovers**   69
Chapter Four   **Sons and Ghosts**   103
Chapter Five   **After the Books**   121

Conclusion   137

Notes   147
Bibliography   171
Index   187
Acknowledgments   197
About the Author   199

Introduction

On a February weeknight in 1956, in Santa Barbara, California, Linda Millar, sixteen and already chronically sad, sat alone in her car and steadily drank nearly two quarts of wine. Then she started driving. She ran through three thirteen-year-old boys walking home from a basketball game at their middle school, Our Lady of Guadalupe. Two of the boys were thrown seventy feet: one of them died and the other was maimed. Linda didn't stop. Ten minutes later she plowed into a parked car with its lights on and a couple inside. That vehicle was thrown sixty feet, and Linda's car rolled over. When she was detained, she lied; it took her forty-eight hours to admit to both accidents. A month afterward, she slashed her wrists and was hospitalized.[1] In June Linda was found guilty on two felony counts and sent to the prison hospital in Camarillo, California.[2] Ken Millar (pronounced "Miller"), her father, was undone.

Millar, using the pseudonym Ross Macdonald, wrote popular detective novels, six with Lew Archer as the detective by 1956. Now he would write something very different. "Notes of a Son and Father" is an unpublished, confessional, harrowing account of Macdonald's childhood, marriage, and fatherhood. It can be found among the Kenneth and Margaret Millar Papers in the Special Collections and

Archives at the University of California at Irvine Libraries. It looks unassuming: a dime-store spiral notebook with thirty-seven un-numbered pages of small, tightly penciled handwriting. Without doubt, it was an anguished exercise in courage both for Macdonald to write and then to give over to researchers who happen across it. It is a keystone of sorts for this book.

Macdonald began writing "Notes of a Son and Father" for Linda's psychiatrist in order to provide "enough to give a line, at least a line to read between."[3] He was desperate to help his child, to heal her faster. "[W]e are interested in the moral mechanisms of family life, and where the machine broke down,"[4] he said. As he worked, he found the process of writing "Notes of a Son and Father" was an accounting of his own life, helpful for his own sake. On every page, Macdonald judges himself guilty of not loving his mother, father, wife, or daughter enough. The reader sees differently: Macdonald's father was unavailable to his son for years at a time; his mother was a hysteric; and his wife was angry. Macdonald—a successful academic and writer, an effortful husband and father—surely loved all of them enough.

Macdonald's childhood was full of predatory secrets and sexual shame. As soon as he could—and by 1936 both his parents had died—Macdonald reinvented himself. He triumphed in this willed performance for twenty years and then his daughter killed a thirteen-year-old boy. So Macdonald wrote "Notes of a Son and Father" and then tried adapting that experience to create openly self-realizing fiction, and the adventure of doing that made him a less-haunted, more present man. He finally could write about his past in the guise of Freudian fables within the structure of the hard-boiled genre. These later books, and particularly the best ones—*The Galton Case*, *The Chill*, and *The Underground Man*—got Macdonald to the far side of pain, to a place where he could make the best of the rest of his life. He changed. His detective changed. As Macdonald would say: "*Solve* is the wrong word. Let's say *understand*."[5] "I think [my novels] have deepened my understanding of life," Macdonald would maintain. "Let's put it this way, my novels have made me into a novelist."[6]

The twelve Lew Archer books written after 1956 extend the work begun by Dashiell Hammett, who invented hard-boiled detective fiction, and Raymond Chandler, who gave it romantic voice. Macdonald's contribution was to see that the genre has conventions that can support any number of themes—yes, even Freudian fables. He also had an inchoate theory that a culture has to have a popular fiction in order to grow an elevated literature, and that's what Hammett, Chandler, and Macdonald did: they turned their work in the hard-boiled, pulp genre into exceptional literature.

Macdonald correctly argues that Dashiell Hammett's work showcases "the direct meeting of art and contemporary actuality" and begins "to find a language and a shape for that experience."[7] Hammett makes clear the "second city," where the secret meanings of the factual world are. He does more than select telling details about San Francisco in 1929; he distills its rank perfume, using its cockeyed vocabulary and inventing the lonely, near-tragic

> little man going forward day after day through mud and blood and death and deceit—as callous and brutal and cynical as necessary towards a dim goal, with nothing to push or pull him towards it except he's been hired to reach it.[8]

Hammett's "little man" is the Continental Op, the first hard-boiled narrating hero. He sprang from the reports Hammett filed as a Pinkerton National Detective Agency operative. From the Op forward, the hard-boiled private eye has been fashioned anomalously in his creator's image, which makes knowing that author's biography all the more crucial to understanding his fiction. In *Self-Portrait: Ceaselessly into the Past*, Macdonald encourages us to coordinate the work with the life:

I can think of few more complex critical enterprises than dis-
entangling the mind and life of a first-person detective story
writer from the mask of his detective-narrator. The assumption
of the mask is as public as vaudeville but as intensely private
as a lyric poem. It is like taking an alias, . . . and it constitutes
among other things an act of identification with the people
one is writing for.[9]

Hammett's coming of age—his Pinkerton work, tuberculosis,
marriage, daughters (and a paternity question that arose in 1980,
nineteen years after Hammett's death), and his long affair with Lillian
Hellman—provided the parts at hand that he used to assemble a
code for both his fictional protagonists and his own behavior. The
code was existentialist, honorable, atheistic, and unexplained; and
it worked for the lot of them—author and shamuses—but not in a
sustained way because it did not address the anxieties that fueled
Hammett's capacity for self-destructive behavior. Readers of his
novels learn more about Hammett than he ever would have wanted
known. They reveal what he and his detective heroes wouldn't dis-
cuss, matters especially taken up in *Red Harvest*, his "sex stories,"
and *The Thin Man*. It's like reading Macdonald's "Notes of a Son
and Father" and seeing what Macdonald doesn't.

In his essay "The Writer as Detective Hero," Macdonald recognizes that this proclaimed-versus-hidden-in-plain-sight model is
also at play, though in different ways, in Raymond Chandler's uses
of his detective Philip Marlowe:

It is Marlowe's doubleness that makes him interesting: the
hard-boiled mask half-concealing Chandler's poetic and
satiric mind. Part of our pleasure derives from the interplay
between the mind of Chandler and the voice of Marlowe.[10]

Chandler elevated the language and the hero of the hard-boiled form.
Macdonald said that he "wrote like a slumming angel, and invested

the sun-blinded streets of Los Angeles with a romantic presence."[11] Brought up on the classics in English public schools, Chandler made over Hammett's private detective into an unlikely soul—a Depression-era, Los Angeles–based knight errant. Moreover, Marlowe isn't who Chandler really was; Marlowe is who Chandler needed to insist he was. Close readings of Chandler's movie scripts for *Double Indemnity* and *Strangers on a Train*, and of his novel *The Long Goodbye* disclose the sexual doubleness that Chandler was concerned to deny in himself. Somewhere in Chandler—in his childhood, education, or marriage—sexual anxieties were wrought that contributed crucially to the sadness in both Marlowe and Chandler. Factor in as well the too-little-considered, doubled reality that Chandler was regarded as a closeted homosexual by his friends in England while living to all intents and purposes as a heterosexual in the United States.

"A man's fiction," Macdonald believed,

no matter how remote it may seem to be from the realistic or the autobiographical, is very much the record of his particular life. Gradually it may tend to become a substitute for the life, a shadow of the life. . . . As the writer grows older more and more of his energy goes to sustain the shadow.[12]

Hammett and Chandler got what they thought they wanted when readers saw them as perfect doubles of their fictional detectives. It became complicated, though, when they started believing those perceptions themselves. Frantic to maintain the shadows, the personae, they crippled themselves and eventually were unable to write fiction at all.

Hammett and Chandler tried to use the hard-boiled genre to mask their own predicaments: the Op's and Sam Spade's vaunted code makes a virtue of Hammett's lifelong need to live at a self-protective remove. His "sex stories" spell out marriage as a male-neutering institution wherein dominating wives run needy husbands and thereby justified Hammett's indiscriminate womanizing. His detectives' across-the-board, wise-guy attitudes condone Hammett's penchant for abrupt violence and slashing verbal cruelty. Marlowe's poetic loneliness eulogizes Chandler's rigidly constrained marriage. The women as bitches or nymphomaniacs in his writing made Chandler's sweaty nervousness in the company of attractive young women seem sensible, while he wrote enough sadistic homosexuals into his novels to deflect any questions about his own doubled sexuality.

But Hammett and Chandler's defenses actually worked to reveal what they attempted to keep hidden; fiction makes known its author's anxieties. "Like burglars," Macdonald writes, "who secretly wish to be caught, we leave our fingerprints on the broken locks, our voice-prints in the bugged rooms, our footprints in the wet concrete and the blowing sand."[13] Given this sense of the failure of every defense and disguise, Macdonald was to read Hammett and Chandler as confessional writers, even when they were trying not to be.

In *Literary Biography*, critic Leon Edel posits an

> axiom that the poem is the poet's and no one else's; the words, the structure, the poem's character and psychology issue from the poet's inner consciousness; its contents are tissued out of those memories of reading and of life that have be-come emotionally charged. In saying this we reject the old and rather naïve concept of the happy artistic inspiration which just "flew" *into* the poet's mind. The flight is outward, from assimilated experience.[14]

Edel's axiom, "flight is outward," is in keeping with psychoanalytic thought; his metaphor is apt for the dispersed power of any man's private sexuality. In *The Novels of Ross Macdonald*, Michael Kreyling emphasizes that we do not develop sexually or psychologically in isolation:

[F]or better or worse we develop in families: the first "others" we desire are family members; the first "others" from whom we hide those desires are the same people. Family tensions ripple outward from the intimate nuclear family to the extended family of kin to the past and future.[15]

Reading literary biography, watching the experience become assimilated, can be a part of truly knowing a work of fiction. Sigmund Freud biographer Ernest Jones's opinion is clear:

A work of art is too often regarded as a finished thing-in-itself, something almost independent of the creator's personality, as if little would be learned about the one or the other by connecting the two studies. Informed criticism, however, shows that a correlated study of the two sheds lights in both directions, on the inner nature of the composition and on the creative impulse of its author. The two can be separated only at the expense of diminished appreciation, whereas to increase our knowledge of either automatically deepens our understanding of the other.[16]

Macdonald fully invites his reader, his critic, to participate in such a correlated study of his novels. He uses the genre straightforwardly; unlike the agendas of Hammett and Chandler, Macdonald's is unhidden. Writing hard-boiled fiction is how he organizes his search for a defined self. His process is something like this: a private, original sin becomes a myth, and that myth is then told within hard-boiled conventions. In this way, Macdonald gets both distance from and perspective on that early, searing pain. "The whole apparatus and tradition of the detective story," he says, "is to provide what I once described as a welder's mask which enables you to handle dangerously hot material."[17]

Macdonald pushes further: he believes that fiction has to have that higher purpose.

> [It] has to feed the writer as he is writing or it won't feed other people. It has to be a living act, which you do for your own sake in your own time. You don't just do it to produce a book. You do it to struggle with demons, to get them under control. I say demons, but I mean problems, memories, or whatever else makes up one's own psychic life. To put it another way, you're wrestling with your own angels.[18]

Macdonald is choosing a welter of sexually tinged metaphors to describe the process of writing fiction: "dangerously hot materials," "feeding [both] the writer [and] other people"; "problems, memories—whatever else makes up one's own psychic life; wrestling with your own angels." These all speak to the guilty anxieties of childhood.

Edel continues, "Art is the result not of calm and tranquility, however much the artist may, on occasion, experience calm in the act of writing. It springs from tension and passion, from a state of disequilibrium in the artist's being."[19] Creative work comes out of the novelist's private and painful history. The process of writing self-realizing fiction assimilates experience for the courageous author and the brave reader. It brings surcease in the forms of understanding and acceptance: "exile and half-recovery and partial return," as Macdonald puts it.[20]

Hence, the solving of the murder case posed in a Hammett, Chandler, or Macdonald novel is nearly beside the point. The real mysteries, those that gain the reader something, are in the several doublenesses: detective and author; coded behaviors and revealed truth; and factual city and second city. Macdonald, in contradistinction to Chandler and Hammett, argues in favor of figuring out the real mysteries above: author, revealed truth, and second city.

The connections between the work and the life—other men's as well as my own—have always interested me. It becomes more and more evident that novels . . . are built like Robinson Crusoe's cabin out of the flotsam of the author's past and his makeshift present.[21]

The more we know of an author's life, the better we can find him in his canon.

Remember that Ross Macdonald is, in effect, telling us: I consciously have started with the secret blows of my childhood, transformed them into myths, and organized those myths into narratives controlled by the conventions of hard-boiled fiction. That Macdonald was and wanted to be engaged in confessional self-analysis when writing his novels is one argument of my book. That Hammett and Chandler were similarly engaged while adamantly not wanting to be is my other contention.

Writing fiction, and perhaps particularly writing hard-boiled novels, is a dynamic undertaking, a living act. It is open-ended: each time the novelist works on his manuscript, the experience, the doing, reveals more. A novel is always a work-in-progress; at some arbitrary point it is called done, abandoned by its author, and published. In an interview, Canadian journalist Jerry Tutunjian accused Macdonald of writing the same story twelve times. His response was, "No. Every time you do it, you dig deeper. It's like going to a shrink: you're discovering different aspects of it, and of yourself."[22] "It's all one case," Macdonald told Paul Nelson of *Rolling Stone*.[23]

For readers, the experience is analogous: each time one approaches a novel, one is slightly different because the reader is a work-in-progress too. At each reading, one sees more and sees differently. The participating, aware reader is learning how, and at what cost, a grounded, integrated life can be self-won. That process is of use to one's own self-awareness, one's own relief. Moreover, the reader's experience does not stop when the novel does; the creative process can lead outward and beyond. The speculating reader is the necessary third party to the author and his hard-boiled, narrating detective—the one who completes the act of identification.

Chapter One
Sons and Fathers

When Linda at only sixteen killed a thirteen-year-old boy, Macdonald was stopped in his tracks, thrown back on his own beginnings. "My half-suppressed Canadian youth and childhood rose like a corpse from the bottom of the sea," he said.[1] Macdonald, heretofore self-reinvented and an intensely private man, underwent Freudian analysis.

In 1948, hoping to make money, Macdonald had written his first Lew Archer novel, but in 1956 and 1957 he wrote *The Doomsters* hoping to make himself well or, as he was learning to accept, well enough. Written during the early days of Macdonald's psychoanalysis, it was his first try at a new kind of hard-boiled writing. The book is about sons and fathers, specifically Carl Hallman, on the lam from a mental hospital, who hires Archer to figure out the suspicious deaths of his wealthy parents. Carl holds himself the "real" cause of his parents' death: his mother's suicide and his father's heart attack right after he argued with the old man. As the plot plays out, it is Hallman's wife who murdered her in-laws, and she did it for security, for money. About sex with her husband, she says,

I'd be in two parts, a hot part and a cold part, and the cold
part would rise up like a spirit. Then I'd imagine that I was
in bed with a golden man. He was putting gold in my purse,
and I'd invest it and make a profit and reinvest. Then I'd feel
rich and real, and the spirit would stop watching me.[2]

For women in Macdonald's later fiction, sexual desire, like murder,
is really a felt need for something else. Indeed, in all his fiction—
and all of Hammett and Chandler's too—"good" women have sex to
get love, and "bad" women are using sex or murder or both to get
money. What both types of women want is security. For that matter,
virtually all the murderers in all three writers' books are women, the
only exception being Hammett's *The Dain Curse*, wherein the killer
is a male novelist.

Macdonald is covering too much ground in *The Doomsters*, with
the result that characters are closer to caricatures. He also succumbs
to the temptation of providing too much autobiographical information
about Archer, which contradicts the role Macdonald now wanted for
him, telling an English interviewer, "He is a deliberately narrowed
version of the writing self."[3] The last misstep is Macdonald's talky
explanation at the novel's end, which is only tenuously connected to
the plot:

I'd guess . . . that she's borderline schizophrenic. Probably
she's been in-and-out of it for several years. . . . she must
have considerable ego strength to have held herself together
for so long. But the crisis could push her back into very deep
withdrawal.[4]

The Doomsters' first theme is the price of denying one's past;
Macdonald, who had "successfully" reinvented himself after the death
of his parents twenty years earlier, had come to a sad realization. "It

isn't possible to brush people off, let alone yourself," Archer says. "They wait for you in time."[5] And he says,

> An alternating current of guilt ran between her and all of us involved with her. . . . Even the Hallman family, the four victims, had been in a sense the victimizers too. The current of guilt flowed in a closed circuit if you traced it far enough.[6]

As a consequence, Macdonald wants to talk about guilty families and scapegoating:

> You know, when a person breaks down, he doesn't do it all by himself. It's something that happens to whole families. The terrible thing is when one member cracks up, the rest so often make a scapegoat out of him. They think they can solve their own problems by rejecting the sick one—locking him up and forgetting him.[7]

Macdonald's guilty sense of pain and culpability in his daughter's breakdown are palpable in *The Doomsters*. But he's moving too fast and slightingly, and hasn't yet learned to explain by implication. Michael Kreyling sums up:

> The protracted denouement of *The Doomsters* serves an extra-literary purpose. Macdonald had personal investments in the psychoanalytic process, and he had pledged his fiction to pay. *The Doomsters* is a split attempt to cover both debts: to mobilize an enormous mass of Freudian material circulating in the atmosphere of the times and in his personal situation to heal his own broken family, and to fulfill his formal obligations to the detective novel. *The Doomsters* left a balance due on both accounts.[8]

The Galton Case was next and better: the author tightens his focus to a son's journey back home after exile from the family, and Macdonald is sure-footed enough to let the action and Archer carry his themes. Connections twist Macdonald's autobiography and classical and psychoanalytic archetypes into a story organized by hard-boiled conventions. The danger is of emotional pain and the courage needed is psychological. It was his breakthrough novel.

The Galton Case, set in real time (1958), starts with a rich client hiring a private detective named Lew Archer; wealthy Californian Maria Galton is dying and wants to reconcile with her son, Anthony ("Tony"). It was 1936 when he angrily left home, dropped out of college, married his working-class, pregnant girlfriend ("Teddy"), and disappeared.

It is too late: Archer follows a poem, "Luna," that Tony wrote in Luna Bay, where he learns that Tony was murdered the same year he disappeared. The search changes: find the baby. Soon enough a twenty-two-year-old man named John Brown Jr. shows up, claiming he's Mrs. Galton's grandson. But it comes to nothing: John Brown Jr. turns out to be Theodore Fredericks, son of a Canadian murderer, and mixed up with a crooked lawyer in a scheme to get the old lady's money.

Then the above facts are overridden: Theodore Fredericks, pretending to be John Galton, really is John Galton. Archer goes to Canada and finds Teddy Fredericks, who tells him that Nelson Fredericks murdered her husband, Tony Galton, took her and her baby, and fled to Canada, where Nelson and Teddy lived as man and wife, and the baby was called Theodore Fredericks.

Macdonald freely imprints himself on this novel: he and John Galton were born near San Francisco, were taken to Canada at very young ages by their mothers, and "Luna" is a poem Macdonald wrote when he was sixteen. Macdonald and John Galton both suffered abusive childhoods. On that private level, Macdonald's childhood and this novel about it are sordid, personal histories of sons and lost fathers.

Macdonald amplifies that same history into a fairy tale told to a very young John Galton by his mother:

> I was only a toddler, and I used to think it was a fairy tale. I realize now it was a story about myself. She wanted me to know about myself, but she was afraid to come right out with it.
>
> She said that I was a king's son, and we used to live in a palace in the sun. But the young king died and the bogeyman stole us away to the caves of ice where nothing was nice. She made a sort of rhyme of it. And she showed me a gold ring with a little red stone set in it that the king had left her for a remembrance.[9]

The mother's fairy tale echoes an earlier description of Maria Galton's estate in palatial terms: "high masonry walls," "stone gateposts in which the name of Galton was cut," "majestic iron gates," "a portcullis effect." "The windows were narrow and deep in the thick walls, like the windows of a medieval castle."[10]

The final passage continues: John Galton describes murdering his false father: "I got a butcher knife out of the drawer, and hid it upstairs in my room. When Fredericks tried to lock me in, I stabbed him in the guts. I thought I'd killed him. By the time I saw a newspaper and found that I hadn't, I was across the border."[11]

This too connects back to an earlier chapter, wherein a minor character remarks, "It sounds like one of the Grimm's fairy tales. The goatherd turns out to be the prince in disguise. Or like Oedipus. John had an Oedipus theory of his own, that Oedipus killed his father because he banished himself from the kingdom."[12]

Oedipus did not knowingly kill his father or marry his mother. In fact, he tried hard not to do these things. Moreover, Oedipus hadn't a choice; he did what he was fated to do. His parents were the more culpable inasmuch as they had banished their son when he was a baby. Yet it is he, the innocent son, who is undone by guilt. *The Galton Case* is an inflation of Macdonald's anger and shame over his own father's death: he didn't protect me from my mother; when he left, we had to leave California and live in Canada; I didn't go with him when he wanted me to; I didn't love him enough.

Elevating the story into alignment with familiar myths serves two purposes: it models how family histories are encrypted and passed, parent to child; and it makes one son's loss applicable to everyone, helpful to everyone. Macdonald's art was expressing something potentially universal. As he said in an interview: "We all eventually lose our fathers. . . . For the reader as well as for the writer, fiction is a handling of pain, not just succumbing to it, but a handling of it, making something better than it was otherwise."[13]

The words "handling" and "making something better" are part and parcel of Macdonald's thinking about the past. The structure-by-elevation is how Macdonald handles and makes something better of his own history. In *The Galton Case*, Macdonald organizes the facts of his own lost father into wider patterns: psychological archetype, classical legend, and fairy tale. Macdonald didn't write himself well, but he did write himself better. Readers can do it too: they safely can locate their childhood inchoate outrage and humiliation in *The Galton Case's* all-encompassing tropes.

The Galton Case plot is a series of repeating stories: a murder that took place a generation ago connects to a murder now; misidentifications beget correct identifications (John Galton becomes Theodore Fredericks becomes John Galton); and second chances abound as a twenty-two-year-old son is lost and a twenty-two-year-old grandson appears.

"I was across the border" should really be "I was back across the border." With its theme of repetition, *The Galton Case* attacks the very American premise that a man can reinvent himself. Theodore Fredericks—and Macdonald—have left cold Canada, "the caves of ice," come to "a palace in the sun," and changed their names. It is a

California cheat: neither John Galton nor Ross Macdonald has outrun his own history. "The California escapists of my books," Macdonald writes elsewhere, "drag with them their whole pasts, rattling like chains among the castanets."[14]

So the work becomes a process of apology and forgiveness. In *The Galton Case*, Maria Galton's forgiving her son for leaving school, marrying against her wishes, and stealing from her, and her felt apology for treating him too harshly set in motion all the action of the novel. And it ends when John Galton and his mother forgive each other:

> "Too much water under the bridge. I don't blame my son for hating me."
> "I don't hate you," John said. "I'm sorry for you, Mother. And I'm sorry for what I said."[15]

In Macdonald's later novels, Archer is judgmental only when a child is suffering or in danger. Thus in *The Galton Case*, he understands Teddy's choosing to remain with her murdering husband out of loneliness: "I had nobody else left in my life excepting him," she tells John. "Don't be too hard on your mother,"[16] Archer says. Understand and accept, Macdonald is arguing, and then move on into the present before it's too late. John Galton has Sheila, who loves him; "Just take good care of your girl,"[17] his mother begs. *The Galton Case* ends hopefully:

> Somewhere outside, a single bird raised its voice for a few notes, then fell into abashed silence. I went to the window. The river was white. The trees and buildings on its banks were resuming their colors and shapes. A light went on in one of the other houses. As if at this human signal, the bird raised its voice again.
> Sheila said: "Listen."

John turned his head to listen. Even the dead man seemed
to be listening.[18]

Tony Galton and his son John are *The Galton Case*'s central
characters, even though Tony has been dead for a generation when
the novel begins and the son has no memory of his lost father. *The
Chill* looks harder at sons and mothers and *The Underground Man*
at sons and other women, but sons and fathers are always there too
at the core of any late Macdonald novel. *The Chill*'s Alex Kincaid
is old enough to get married but emotionally undercut by his father.
Alex does what his father demands, abandons his new wife in a
mental hospital and returns home to his parents, but the next day he
moves out and returns to his bride, telling Archer:

When Dad gets upset it has a peculiar effect on me. It's like
sympathetic vibrations: he goes to pieces, I go to pieces. Not
that I'm blaming *him*. . . . Dad's afraid he can't adjust, and I
guess it makes him afraid of things in general.

You started me off with what you said about annulling
myself. I felt that way when I went home with Dad.[19]

Then, in the happiest three sentences in Macdonald's canon, Alex
exclaims, "It's really amazing, you know? You really can make a
decision inside yourself. You can decide to be one thing or the
other."[20] Look at what Alex has said: he acknowledges the power his
childhood has over him, sees the repetition of his father in himself,
and thereby moves on. This is the fundamental process necessary
to mature, mental well-being. Archer thinks, "The only trouble was
that you had to make that decision every hour on the hour. But he
would have to find that out for himself."[21]

In *The Underground Man*, Stanley Broadhurst's father disappeared
when he was twelve, and Stanley obsessively looks for him, to the

extent of shortchanging his six-year-old son. At the novel's end there is a murdered son buried in the same grave as his murdered father, two father substitutes, and two surviving, fatherless boys. But there is a third fatherless boy—a boy-like man, actually. Perhaps Macdonald was thinking about him when, in his last novel, *The Blue Hammer*, he has Archer realize: "My chosen study was other men, hunted men in rented rooms, aging boys clutching at manhood before night fell and they grew suddenly old."[22] That boy, those men, are who Macdonald grieves for most, because they beg the Oedipal question: what happens if the son wins?

Ross Macdonald eventually puzzled out the connection of his father to his own manhood. In his crucial autobiographical document, "Notes of a Son and Father," he refers to himself as "the son," with his mother named "the son's mother," his wife "the son's wife," and his daughter "the son's daughter": Macdonald is consistently referencing his relationship as a son to John "Jack" Macdonald Millar. "I was my wandering father's son, after all, . . . even though I saw him infrequently, sometimes not for years at a time,"[23] said Macdonald.

Millar and his wife, Anna Moyer, separated when their son, Kenneth Millar (Macdonald), was four years old. And there it is: the son had won, and because the triumph felt sexual, Macdonald experienced the loss of his father as guilt: "My original sin, so to speak, was to be left by my father."[24] Misplaced guilt, like misidentifications, is strongly present in Macdonald's fiction.

Millar was "a futile Ulysses, a Jack London with more heart and less brains," Macdonald wrote. Millar was forty-one, writing poetry, and working as a harbor pilot in Vancouver Harbor when his son was born in 1915. He had been a wrestler and long-distance swimmer, lived with the Indians of Vancouver Island, helped the Japanese and Chinese during the 1907 Vancouver anti-immigration riots, started three newspapers, and suffered a minor stroke. Macdonald loved to remember one crucially golden day:

One of those days still seems the happiest day of my childhood if not my life. I mean the unforgettable day when my
father first took me to sea in a harbor boat, and I stood beside
him in the offshore light, with his hands and my hand on the
wheel.[25]

After the separation, Jack Millar wandered:

[E]ast and west he traveled, still on the trail of a wished-for
world where Indians and white men shared the unploughed
territories or climbed through the blowing passes to the north.
Though my father's life was more adventurous, and less prosperous, I became aware at almost every turn that it was
patterned on *his* father's life, just as my own recurrences to
the west and north have been patterned on my father's.[26]

Anna took her boy back to Ontario, Canada, where she did badly
and Macdonald, referring to himself as "the son," had guilty feelings
about his father:

His son spent his life trying to forgive him his bad luck; part
of which consisted in his marrying a woman unfit for marriage.
And the son has spent his life trying to unlearn the habit of
self-pity, which so often can end in nihilism or diabolism. But
has not.[27]

Relatives helped him here and there. A second cousin, Rob
Millar, and his wife, Elizabeth, took Macdonald in when he was six
years old. While living with them, Macdonald later wrote, labeling
himself "the boy," he bullied playmates, repeatedly physically
seduced "a mentally retarded nineteen-year-old 'maid,'" and began
a habit of stealing:

The earliest theft occurred in this period. The cousin had lost two young daughters and kept their pictures in an Indian basket, with other mementos, including some silver money. The boy stole a dime of this silver and used it to buy a ten-cent pencil, which he broke deliberately in his hands soon after leaving the store.[28]

Maybe because he felt both guilty about and angry at his father, while in the home of a father figure who seemed to love him, Macdonald did things to earn guilt again: insecure things (stealing and breaking reminders of Rob's "real" daughters) and enraged, sexual things. He was only eight years old when his time with Rob and Elizabeth— "the most fortunate thing that ever happened in my life"[29]—was over. Rob's wife died unexpectedly—Macdonald remembered the evening—and Rob said he couldn't keep him.

By age eleven, Macdonald was getting into more trouble: "petty theft, a few homosexual episodes with other boys, some fights in which the thought of the father's failure was involved." But, Macdonald added, "This thought also helped to cause the boy to head his class in both studies and athletics."[30] And that's the irony: anxiety can create rigid "successes": good grades, playing sports in an all-out style.

Macdonald was twelve when his father came to see him; Millar shyly and uncertainly proposed that the two of them go out west on one last adventure. Macdonald turned him down, and thereafter the self-destructive behaviors ramped up: he drank, fought, and "the patterns of theft and homosexuality made him miserable."[31]

At thirteen Macdonald went to live with an aunt and her husband, "a cold Pharisee of a man," Macdonald would later say. "They rejected the boy at the end of the year, no doubt for good reason. There was no theft this year, but homosexual episodes continued and I believe one came to their attention, though they never spoke of it."[32]

Jack Millar was, Macdonald wrote, "visited by the son, who was ashamed of him and also loved him, but not enough."[33] Now permanently hospitalized in charity wards after a series of strokes, Millar couldn't speak, but he was still writing poetry in couplets. Macdonald hitchhiked to see Rob Millar, but Rob had remarried and had a "real son" now; Macdonald spent the night and left.

Macdonald left high school at sixteen and got a job offering room and board with a (Canadian) Pennsylvania Dutch farm family "who treated him like a son. In the first month of it, he made the conscious decision never to steal again, and with a single exception two years later, this was the end of the homosexual episodes."[34] It is the same irony: in response to guilt and anger, Macdonald developed will and put his faith in it—and it all looked like success for a long time.

It was while Macdonald was working on that farm that Jack Millar died. He left his only child his personal copy of Henry David Thoreau's *Walden*; the proceeds—$2,012—of a life insurance policy came to Anna Millar, and she gave it to their son. Macdonald was eighteen years old and had enough money to go to college. "Before I reached University," Macdonald wrote, "looking around for something to become in my father's absence, I had become a writer."[35]

So in his later and best novels, Macdonald refigures his childhood experience of his own father. He elevates that pain to a universal level by describing that experience in the vocabulary of classical myths and psychological archetypes.

Greek legends are stories about families: that's what made referencing them a powerful choice on Macdonald's part. "Here we have the fundamental structural flaw in the Greek family," Philip E. Slater writes in *The Glory of Hera: Greek Mythology and the Greek Family.*

> Within the family circle the thin patriarchal veneer tends to collapse, and the child does not experience paternal adequacy where it is needed. Indeed, Heracles is soon struck by the

same insight, protesting that all of his glorious deeds are point-
less if he is incapable of fulfilling the most elementary male
role—protecting his wife and children.[36]

Freudian psychoanalysis, as it was generally practiced in 1950s
America (when Macdonald was being treated), postulates that for
every son—not just those with fathers present—there is a necessary
progression of tasks. The little boy, who is infatuated with his
mother, resents his father's presence as her lover and often fanta-
sizes about violently getting rid of his father. Analogously, the male
child fears his father: "The same part is played by the father alike
in the Oedipus and the castration complexes," writes Sigmund Freud
in *Totem and Taboo: Resemblances Between the Mental Lives of Savages
and Neurotics*—"the part of dreaded enemy to the sexual interests
of childhood. The punishment which he threatens is castration, or
its substitute, blinding."[37] In *The Interpretation of Dreams*, Freud
explains the universal power of *Oedipus Rex* or similarly themed
literary works:

> His destiny moves us only because it might have been ours—
> because the oracle laid the same curse upon us before our
> birth as upon him. It is the fate of all of us, perhaps, to direct
> our first sexual desire towards our mother and our first hatred
> and our first murderous wish against our father.[38]

So goes the paradigm, one Macdonald would adapt in significant
ways.

Psychologist Michael Kahn reiterates Freud's point:

> We have seen how crucial it is that children do not become
> convinced they have won the Oedipal struggle, and how impor-
> tant it is that parents maintain a constant position that there
> is no possibility of the child winning. . . . In the realm of

primary process the wish, for example the wish to kill, is
equivalent to the act, and exile is equivalent to murder.[39]

All of this—the stuff of classical myth, modern psychoanalysis, and
Macdonald's childhood experience—is the source of inescapable
and unearned guilt and one of the concerns of Macdonald's last,
best Archer novels. And remember: every son is Oedipus, and all
fathers do go missing. "I have an idea," Macdonald says,

> that the bad things that happen to people, misfortunes and
> sorrows, are only bad so long as you don't convert them into
> something better. It's been my experience in life that a very
> bad thing, if you survive it and learn from it, you're better
> off than you were in the first place. This is for me the way
> life works and one of the experiences of life is loss followed
> by recovery, and this is particularly true of a novelist. It's
> undoubtedly one of the reasons I became one. A novelist has
> the ability to go back, clear to the beginnings of his life and
> his troubles and his sorrows, and convert them into some-
> thing that will not only be pleasing and satisfying to him, but
> also meaningful to other people.[40]

"Convert": this is how a writer works through the most fundamental
and private difficulties in his life—and invites self-realizing readers
to do the same. *The Galton Case* ends with John and his dead father
listening. Lew Archer is more listener than solver, just as a book's
reader listens to its author.

Macdonald consistently chooses to use the conventions of genre
American detective fiction to tell his stories of sons and fathers. His
novels come not only from his autobiography and his study of psychology, literature, and myths, but also from the men whose hard-boiled
novels prefigured his own, Dashiell Hammett and Raymond Chandler.
Hammett and Chandler insisted that they were not autobiographical

writers, but in some ways they were. Their own fathers didn't matter, they said; that's why they didn't talk about them or write about them. But of course they mattered. The reader of Macdonald's late novels is best served by understanding those similarly anxious hard-boiled novelists, Hammett and Chandler, who came before.

O ne fictional father figure is writ large in Hammett's canon. His two most sustained characters are an operative for the Continental Detective Agency and his boss: the Continental Op and the Old Man. This state of affairs mirrors Hammett-the-writer and Hammett-the-son: in each, the father figure matters more than the actual father.

The Op appears in thirty-six stories and two novels, and it is always his Old Man who launches him into the adventure at hand. The Op/Old Man relationship has three aspects, the first being that the Op acts more like an adolescent son than an employee dealing with his boss. He says, for example, that the Old Man will give him "merry hell, . . . will boil me in oil if he ever finds out what I've been doing."[41] At the end of *Red Harvest*, he confesses, "I spent most of my week in Ogden trying to fix up my reports so they would not read as if I had broken as many Agency rules, state laws, and human bones as I had."[42]

Second, the Op is at pains to describe just how tough his Old Man is. For "The Scorched Face," he is drawn as "The Old Man, with his gentle eyes behind gold spectacles and his mild smile, hiding the fact that fifty years of sleuthing had left him without any feelings at all on any subject."[43] This picture is reinforced in "The Big Knockover":

Fifty years of crook-hunting for the Continental had emptied him of everything except brains and a softspoken shell of polite- ness that was the same whether things were good or bad—

and meant as little at one time as another. We who worked under him were proud of his cold-bloodedness. We used to boast that he could spit icicles in July, and we called him Pontius Pilate among ourselves, because he smiled politely when he sent us out to be crucified on suicidal jobs.[44]

This, then, is the role model: a man with no name, just a function. He is without affect, unforthcoming, nothing but code.

Third, the Op/Old Man dynamic changes as the Op gains experience. The Old Man trusts him more; in "Fly Paper,"

The Old Man gave me the telegram and a check, saying: "You know the situation. You'll know how to handle it." I pretended to agree with him.[45]

In the later Op novel, *The Dain Curse*, and the last four Op short stories, the Op is beginning to be a father figure himself; he is supervising other, less seasoned operatives. The Old Man tacitly acknowledges the Op as a grown son. Hammett and his own father never got that far.

Samuel Dashiell Hammett was a country baby, born on May 27, 1894, at home on his paternal grandfather's Maryland farm. Before his time, there had been a town called Hammettville on the Patuxent River, where his great-grandfather had lived. Twenty-seven Hammetts are indexed in *History of St. Mary's County, Maryland*, which was written, appropriately enough, by Regina Combs Hammett in 1977.[46] Descendants of Hammett's brother Richard are there now. Another Samuel Hammett of St. Mary's County, Maryland, was killed in the First World War.

His paternal tribe's multitudes and history aside, Hammett experienced family life as counterfeit and anxious. His parents were unhappy, and his mother, Anne Hammett, née Dashiell, encouraged the three children to believe that their father, Richard, was the problem. He appears never to have caught hold of a profession, and, as time went on and his various dreams didn't pan out, he began to seem like a braggart and a fraud. In his own adulthood, Hammett would be adamantly honest, frequently to the point of rudeness, and ruthlessly self-critical, often to his own emotional detriment. Hammett's early relationship with his father was stormy and, when the young man moved away from home and got beyond asking for money, their connection became tenuous. Hammett's father never left his family, but Hammett left him; while remaining close to his mother and sister, he would go eight years without seeing Richard in the 1930s and would have no communication with his brother, also named Richard, for more than twenty years.

Still, there were aspects of his father that Hammett must have sneakily appreciated: the elder Hammett had ward-heeling tendencies and was a snappy dresser; his niece remembered his appearing "in St. Mary's County in cars driven by attractive women in their mid thirties" and dressed "just like the governor of Maryland himself." He "caroused, consorting with beauticians, whom he seemed to favor, drinking heavily."[47] Hammett was openly admiring when Richard in his later life had to have a leg amputated and thereafter took up rhumba dancing.[48] Hammett paid for his father's funeral but didn't attend and then later wished he had. Hammett paid for the artificial leg too.

Richard was an unenthusiastic farmer, so in 1897 the family moved to Philadelphia, where Anne had family and Richard had aspirations. By 1898, they were living in a rented house in Baltimore with Anne's mother. Richard worked as a clerk, salesman, bus conductor, foreman at a lock factory, and dealer in oysters. The family moved in and out of Mrs. Dashiell's house as Richard's paychecks came and went. Anne was the parent with the work ethic; she "went out" as a private nurse. Hammett blamed his ineffectual father for his mother's having to work when she was sick: she "had a chest," as the saying went before anybody said "tuberculosis."

There was an incident somewhere in these years that became telling as Hammett's life played out. He was still small when he hit another boy with a stick, making his chin bleed. The other boy was winning at hockey, which provoked sudden fury from Hammett. In the face of it, he ran, terrified and shamed by what he blindly had done.[49]

The children made their way through Baltimore's public school system. In 1908 Hammett started at Baltimore Polytechnic High School, a special school earmarked for bright students, a place to get ready for college. Hammett got in one semester before his father called a halt: his son was old enough, tall enough, and cocksure enough to work. He was fourteen years old and his formal education was done.

For seven years Hammett worked unhappily and peripatetically, operating a nail machine, running messages for the B & O Railroad, chalking up stock market transactions for the Poe & Davies Brokerage House, and doing other entry-level jobs from which he never went up, only out—quitting or being fired. Hammett was living reluctantly with his parents and siblings in his grandmother's house. He lit out every night, a fledgling man-about-town. He drank, played cards and dice, bet on horses and fights, and frequented every "soiled dove" he found. (Hammett would invent a marvelous soiled dove, the enterprising Dinah Brand, for his first novel, *Red Harvest*.) In summer 1915, a blind ad appeared in the Baltimore paper: "wide work experience and be free to travel and respond to all situations,"[50] orphans preferred. Hammett jumped at the chance and was hired by the Baltimore office of Pinkerton's National Detective Service. He hunted counterfeiters, bank swindlers, jewel thieves, and forgers. The Pinkertons used him as a guard and hotel detective. In 1917 they sent him west to Butte, Montana, to be a strikebreaker during the murderous Anaconda Copper Mining Company strike. (Butte would give him common ground with his wife, the beginnings of a political conscience, and the setting for his first novel.) Now he had adventures; he had stories. Anne and Richard hoped the job would make a man of their son, and it did. Hammett had found his rhythm.

The fun stopped on June 24, 1918, the date Hammett enlisted in the Army. Trained as an ambulance driver, he never got farther than Camp Meade, Maryland. Afterward he was careful to say that he was in the Army at the time of World War I, but he did not fight. There was a second seminal event: Hammett overturned an ambulance and people were hurt. Hammett quietly decided never to drive again, and, except for a very few instances, he didn't.[51] By October he was sick, reportedly felled by the Spanish influenza epidemic of 1918 in which GIs acted as unwitting vectors and 548,000 Americans died.[52] But Hammett was medically discharged from the Army on May 29, 1919, with a different disease: "untreatable tuberculosis."

Thereafter, that diagnosis roiled Hammett's life. TB meant both shame and a death sentence for him, much as HIV/AIDS would sixty years later. Given that TB was spread through the air by coughing, sneezing, and spitting, it was the disease of the urban poor living in crowded squalor. The afflicted coughed chronically, bringing up a mixture of blood, mucus, and saliva that they spit into sputum cups. They had night sweats, infected sores and lesions, and dropped weight until they were skeletal. Landlords in San Francisco had to tell prospective tenants if someone with TB had lived in the apartment. They also could refuse to rent to a "lunger."

In the short run, out of the Army after only eleven months, Hammett went home. He hadn't a choice; he was sick. Beginning at the end of May 1919, Hammett worked intermittently for Pinkerton's Baltimore office. He stuck out life at home for a year and then, in a Hail Mary decision, the twenty-five-year-old transferred to the Pinkerton branch in Spokane, Washington, as far from home as he could get.

With his disease in remission, Hammett went all over the Northwest on Pinkerton business in summer 1920. Somewhere in these years of on-and-off Pinkerton service, a third telling episode happened.

Hammett shot a man. He was guarding an ammunition magazine when a thief started scaling the fence and wouldn't stop when Hammett shouted. Hammett shot him, the man grabbed at himself, dropped off the fence, and ran.[53] Hammett stopped carrying a gun. As was the case when he injured the boy and overturned the ambulance, Hammett was horrified at how easily he could hurt someone; his response was characteristically absolute: he was through with hitting, driving, and shooting for the rest of his life.

In each of the three events, Hammett appears to have been afraid of his own capacity for violence and losing self-control, and he experienced those fears as shame. Like the college student Macdonald, Hammett set rigid rules for himself in response to guilt—and that "worked" until it didn't anymore. The words an older Macdonald would use for getting past shame—"understanding," "acceptance," "forgiveness," "half-recovery and partial return"—did not occur to Hammett. Macdonald is saying that shameful secrets stop being shameful when they stop being secrets. Once acknowledged, the character (or author or reader) finds that his instincts are shared and universal. But Hammett's response was to clamp down, never to speak of what had happened.

Years later, Hammett's anxiety about violence leaked out and into the first Op novel, *Red Harvest*. When he wanted to write a novel of social criticism and political corruption, he set it in Personville— called "Poisonville"—the stand-in for Butte where he had been a Pinkerton strikebreaker in 1917. In *Red Harvest* old Elihu Willsson owns everything: the mining company, the bank, and the newspapers. When the mine was struck, Willsson hired gangsters, and the miners backed down. Now, however, the gangsters are ensconced: one runs all the gambling, another the bootlegging, and a third one organizes thieves and fences. To round it all out, the chief of police is corrupt. Nobody wants to hand Poisonville back to Willsson, so he hires the Continental Detective Agency to get rid of the "mail-order troops." With the agency on the scene, the Op tells Willsson, "You'll get your

city back, all nice and clean and ready to go to the dogs again."[54]
The Op sets the various criminal factions against each other. At novel's
end, twenty-four people have been murdered; Willsson and the Op
are still standing; and that's "success."

There is a phenomenon in law enforcement that Hammett puts
into his first novel: the close relationship between criminal and detective, due to a shared respect for sticking to a code, maintaining
a shell, and toughing it out without complaint. At the end of *Red
Harvest*, the Op admires the way gangster Reno Starkey dies:

> I knew pain had stopped him, but I knew he would go on
> talking as soon as he got himself in hand. He meant to die as
> he had lived, inside the same tough shell. Talking could be
> torture, but he wouldn't stop on that account, not while any-
> body was there to see him. He was Reno Starkey who would
> take anything the world had without batting an eye, and he
> would play it out that way to the end.[55]

Red Harvest is the first time the Op disappoints his code and is
thereby lost. By his own description, he becomes "blood simple,"
beguiled by violence.

> I've arranged a killing or two in my time when they were
> necessary. But this is the first time I ever got the fever. . . .
> Play with murder enough and it gets you in one of two ways.
> It makes you sick, or you get to like it.
> [I]t was easier to have them killed off, easier and surer,
> and now that I'm feeling this way, more satisfying. . . . I looked
> at Noonan and knew he hadn't a chance in a thousand of
> living another day because of what I had done to him, and I
> laughed, and felt warm and happy inside. That's not me.[56]

Or at least he couldn't admit it was.

Look at what has happened here: Hammett is terrified of violence, not so much because he might hurt someone or be hurt himself, but because he might like it. As he comes of age, he makes a code to deny himself that guilty desire: no hitting, no driving, no shooting. When he's twenty-three, Hammett gets sent to Butte as a strikebreaker. He sees Frank Little, the antiwar union leader of International Workers of the World, lynched. Eleven years later, Hammett is still anxious about what he did in Butte and how it felt, so for his first novel he takes his short story hero, the nothing-but-code Op, and sends him to Personville/Poisonville, which is Butte. And, for the first time, code doesn't protect him. Not coincidentally, it is also the first time the Op drinks on the job. This is a Macdonald-like progression: Hammett uses the conventions of hard-boiled fiction to examine his own guilty history. The genre gives him a safe way to talk about what he did and how it felt. Unlike Macdonald, Hammett doesn't have Freud's *Civilization and Its Discontents* to tell him mankind is instinctually aggressive, that his (and his readers') urges are universal. Nor does Hammett necessarily know that he is writing confessional fiction. Twenty-five years after he wrote his first novel, Hammett would be shocked when Senator Joseph McCarthy asked if he advocated the violent overthrow of the United States. *Red Harvest* is dead-serious fiction.

Back in 1920 came the refrain: Hammett got sick again. In November of that year, Hammett met 2nd Lieutenant (she outranked him) Josephine ("Jose," pronounced "Joe's") Dolan at the Cushman Institute, the public health hospital in Tacoma, Washington, that he wound up in when he was too sick to be a Pinkerton.

In 1921 Jose and Hammett moved to San Francisco, got married, had a baby, and Hammett rejoined the Pinkertons for the third time. It was during this tenure that he saw California sleaze in a higher stratum, working for the defense in the trumped-up Fatty Arbuckle rape-and-manslaughter case and for the prosecution in the multiple transgressions of con artist Nicky Arnstein, who had fixed the 1919 World Series and married Fanny Brice.[57]

But the undertow—active, intractable tuberculosis—came back. One can trace Hammett's life through the 1920s by how much he weighed and what percentage of his Army salary the Veteran's Bureau was paying him in disability. By the end of 1921, the 6'2" Hammett weighed 126 pounds and was very sick. He and Jose both thought he was dying. After all, in 1922 more than 70 percent of TB patients in California did die.[58] Hammett couldn't walk from the bedroom to the bathroom without help. Continuing work as a Pinkerton operative was impossible. Freelance writing was the only moneymaking gig Hammett could come up with that could be done in bed. By early 1922, he and Jose were so desperate for money that Hammett wrote to his father, asking for a loan. Richard grudgingly sent some money, along with a refusal to send more and a harangue against freelance work. Then on August 3, 1922, another Hammett did die of tuberculosis: Anne Bond Dashiell Hammett, who had to work while she was sick, died young, and two months before the son she had championed saw his first fiction published. Between the lecturing letter and his mother's death, Hammett was pretty much finished with his father by the end of 1922.

Yet Hammett was happiest in male bastions: the Pinkertons, the Army, the veteran's hospital, *Black Mask* (Joseph T. Shaw's pulp detective magazine), and even prison; the pull of esprit de corps was very real.[59] He must have been open to the possibility of good father figures because he found them. The first was the crusty soul who was assistant superintendent of the Pinkerton's Baltimore office and trained the twenty-one-year-old to be an operative.[60] Jimmy Wright happened along just when Hammett needed him. Here was an adult man who was different from Richard. Operatives adhered to ground rules: don't cheat your client and don't violate your own integrity. Stay anonymous. Operatives aren't identified by name, and reports are filed by number. Stay quiet. Drinking and gambling were forbidden unless needed in an undercover situation.[61] Stay objective. Operatives are on twenty-four-hour call so their code is always in play. For Hammett, who was chary of his emotions and had a strong sense of personal honesty, hated pretense but wanted desperately to have "style," the rules became his code, a way for him to be in the world. "He had found a job that in a sense validated his own need for distance,"[62] writes Sinda Gregory in *Private Investigations: The Novels of Dashiell Hammett.*

Hammett's second father figure was the man who hired him as a copywriter and advertising manager in 1926. Between 1922 and 1926, Hammett had studied journalism at Munson's Business College and had published stories and ephemera in seventeen different pulp magazines and in several genres: "sex," "novelty," "crook," adventure, and western: fully fictional and not based on personal experience. *The Smart Set*, edited by H. L. Mencken and George Jean Nathan, was "a magazine for cleverness." In it, Hammett had published some of his ephemeral pieces and had sold advertising copy he had written. Hammett used a pseudonym for his early work, "Peter Collinson," which was a dig at his father: a "Peter Collins" was a nobody, so Peter Collinson was a nobody's son.

But by 1926 there just wasn't enough money. His daughter, Mary, was in kindergarten and Jose was pregnant. Hammett had to get a job, and he did: as copywriter/advertising manager for Samuels Jewelers, "The House of Lucky Wedding Rings," at $350 a month. Hammett concocted weekly three-hundred-word "essay ads": dramatic stories about people in all sorts of situations finding happiness by buying a Samuels diamond. He blossomed under the structure of a regular job and grew a mustache. The best part was his congenial boss, Albert S. Samuels, "as close to a patron as Hammett ever had," and "upon whom Hammett would fasten if not orphan love, at least wild gratitude."[63] Samuels encouraged him to keep up his freelance writing and predicted great things for him. When Hammett had an affair with a secretary, Samuels made no judgment; when Hammett disappeared on a bender and then reappeared, Samuels took him out to lunch.[64] Hammett started at Samuels in March 1926; two months later his second daughter, Josephine ("Jo"), was born; and two months after that he collapsed at work. He was found lying in a pool of blood, hemorrhaging from his lungs. Hammett was taken again to the veterans' hospital; now he had TB and hepatitis. That summer he and Jose waited again for him to die.

After eight weeks, it was clear Hammett couldn't come back to work. Samuels wrote to the Veterans' Bureau in his behalf, and Hammett was granted complete disability ($100 a month), on condition of his living alone. Four years later, Hammett borrowed $1,000 from Samuels and moved to New York. Hammett would dedicate his fourth novel, *The Dain Curse*, to him. He had worked for Albert Samuels for only five months.

In December 1922, *Black Mask* had published Hammett's first short story; in October 1923, his first Op story appeared. What prefigured the Op's first-person narratives weren't fictional detective stories but rather the recollections of real-life detectives, especially Pinkerton founder Allen Pinkerton's memoirs and Hammett's own "From the Memoirs of a Private Detective," published in March 1923 in *The Smart Set*. The latter article was a numbered list of twenty-nine observations and anecdotes taken from Hammett's experiences as a Pinkerton operative.

A man whom I was shadowing went out into the country for a walk one Sunday afternoon and lost his bearings completely. I had to direct him back to the city.

I was once falsely accused of perjury and had to perjure myself to escape arrest.

I know a man who once stole a Ferris wheel.[65]

Hammett had found his medium, and detective fiction was about to turn a corner: from upper-class amateur detectives with spotless reputations to working-class, hired detectives with average looks, average smarts, and compromised morality; from intricate plots with ingenious resolutions to slammed-through battles ending, at best, in gritty survival. The Op's first-person narratives are elaborated-upon and fictional versions of the reports Hammett filed with the home office when he was a Pinkerton. Hammett's writer-as-witness style was congruent with founder Allen Pinkerton's trademark "eye that never sleeps" and with the emotional detachment that was part of the Op's code.

Pinkerton's ground rules for operatives, the Op's code, and Hammett's stringent, private set of moral principles were all of a piece, and at their core was a demanding work ethic wrought of rigidity in response to unacknowledged fears and guilt. Joseph T. Shaw, *Black Mask*'s editor from 1926 to 1936, recalled Hammett's "unrelenting labor and unflagging perseverance through those early days."[66] Shaw was a national saber champion, a bayonet instructor, and a World War I hero. He was licensed to carry a sword cane. Shaw came at *Black Mask* with enormous energy and confidence:

> We meditated on the possibility of creating a new type of detective story. . . . Obviously, the creation of a new pattern was a writer's rather than an editor's job. Consequently, search was made in the pages of the magazine for a writer with the requisite spark and originality, and we were amazingly encouraged by the promise evident in the work of one.[67]

Mary remembered Shaw coming to their apartment and bringing her a doll. Shaw promised her father higher rates and more creative freedom if he'd write an Op novel, to be published serially in his magazine. Hammett was enthusiastic: "That is exactly what I've been thinking about and working toward. As I see it, the approach

I have in mind has never been attempted. The field is unscratched and wide open."[68] The distinctive authenticity in characterization, action, and dialogue that Hammett was working toward and Shaw was encouraging came to be known first as "The *Black Mask* School" and later as "hard-boiled."

What Hammett and Shaw invented in the 1920s and early 1930s was a very American genre because it is practical; here is how you can make your way in life. At the same time that Ernest Hemingway was writing manuals of instruction, "how to catch a fish," Hammett was penning "how to be a detective." Macdonald's work in the late 1950s until the mid-1970s was also American because it is hopeful, implying "you can get better."

The hard-boiled fiction of a washed-up American/Englishman named Raymond Chandler, who wrote from the late 1930s to the early 1950s, is neither practical nor hopeful.

Hammett's detectives—the Op, Sam Spade, and Nick Charles—were, for good or ill, very much like him, as was Macdonald's Archer, the "understander." It is Chandler's sad and lonely Philip Marlowe, though, who best reveals his author to his reader. Chandler insisted on Philip Marlowe. Although at great pains not to be, Chandler too was a highly confessional writer.

In 1943, when movie business neophyte Chandler collaborated with Hollywood's experienced Billy Wilder to write a screenplay based on James M. Cain's novel *Double Indemnity*, Chandler prevailed in changing the book in a curious way. In Cain's telling, Walter Huff is an amoral, slick insurance agent who meets Phyllis Nirdlinger when he tries to sell her husband car insurance. Huff immediately knows that Phyllis is both highly sexed and capable of murdering her husband without falling apart. Huff believes he has orchestrated the intricate, successful killing of Howard Nirdlinger, only to learn way too late that he has been played by Phyllis, who already had murdered Nirdlinger's first wife and their children. The head of the claims department at General Fidelity of California, a fellow called Keyes, figures out a way to safeguard the company's reputation by putting Huff, under another name, onto a South Seas steamer. But that's a set-up too; Keyes has put Phyllis on the same ship. Huff ends the novel:

> She's made her face chalk white, with black circles under her eyes and red on her lips and cheeks. She's got that red thing on. It's awful-looking. . . . her hands look like stumps underneath it when she moves them around. She looks like what came aboard the ship to shoot dice for souls in "The Rime of the Ancient Mariner."
>
> I didn't hear the stateroom door open, but she's beside me now while I'm writing. I can feel her.
>
> The moon.[69]

In Chandler and Wilder's *Double Indemnity* screenplay, Phyllis, like Neff (his last name was slightly changed), has no criminal history. They are a classic, vivid example of folie à deux, wherein two people only manifest delusional behavior when together. The screenplay stresses the dull price to be paid for moral living. As Wilder put it, "For Walter Neff, crooking the house might be fun."[70] Decency is sterile: Neff sells insurance and Phyllis knits. Murder is erotic:

> Phyllis (describing her dull marriage to an older man): "So I just sit and knit."
> Walter: "That what you married him for?"
> Phyllis: "Maybe I like the way his thumbs hold up the wool."
> Walter (grinning): "Anytime his thumbs get tired. . . . (leering) Only with me around you wouldn't have to knit."

Phyllis: "Wouldn't I?"
Walter: "Bet your life you wouldn't."[71]

The biggest change from the novel to the screenplay is the en-
hanced importance of Keyes, who acquires a first name—Barton—in
the movie. Whereas he outsmarts Huff in Cain's novel, in Chandler's
version Keyes is the emotional center. Wilder biographer Ed Sikov
describes Keyes as

> not only a moral force in the film but also . . . a paternal,
> fraternal, and avuncular character, all in one. . . . he's a figure
> of love—short, chubby, sweating love. . . . Whenever the
> older man fumbles around his jacket pockets searching for
> the matches he never keeps, his younger friend pulls out one
> of his own, flicks it singlehandedly against his thumbnail,
> and provides the missing light. It's a gesture of affection, a
> poignant acknowledgment of one man's need for another.[72]

They light each other up and, in fact, a variation on that gesture
ends the movie:

Neff: "You know why you didn't figure this one, Keyes? Let
me tell you. The guy you were looking for was too close.
He was right across the desk from you."
Keyes: "Closer than that, Walter." (The eyes of the two men
meet in a moment of silence.)
Neff: "I love you too."

Neff fumbles for the handkerchief in Keyes' pocket, pulls it out,
and clumsily wipes his face with it. The handkerchief drops from his
hand. He gets a loose cigarette out of his pocket and puts it between
his lips. Then with great difficulty he gets out a match, tries to strike
it, but is too weak. Keyes takes the match out of his hand, strikes

it for him, and lights his cigarette. The scene fades out.[73] Wilder credited Chandler for the Neff/Keyes relationship:

> *Double Indemnity* was really a love story between two men— Fred MacMurray and Edward G. Robinson, who was Mac-Murray's older co-worker and boss at the insurance agency. Robinson knows that MacMurray is up to no good, and he tries to save him, tries to keep him from going bad and succumbing to the influence of the evil Barbara Stanwyck. A love story between two men . . . That story hadn't really been a part of Cain's novel, but was something added by Ray, who saw the potential there.[74]

Cain said this about the *Double Indemnity* screenplay:

> It's the only picture I ever saw made from my books that had things in it I wish I had thought of. [The] ending was much better than my ending. . . . I would have done it if I had thought of it. There are situations in the movie that can make your hands get wet.[75]

Chandler had thrown the emotional weight of the screenplay behind an ostensible father figure: an older man to look out for a younger one and warn him about women, yet that older man is also a homo-erotic love-object.

Is Chandler's *Double Indemnity* the inverse of his experience of his own father and his parents' relationship? Studied closely, it becomes apparent that Chandler's canon, including *Double Indemnity*, is in part a reactive repetition of his early childhood. Chandler biographer Tom Hiney believes that "Chandler would always be more influenced by having seen the effect of his father's neglect on his mother than he was by Florence herself."[76]

It was a dubious marriage from the start, with little money, railroad work here and there, and the husband's drinking. But after a year there was a baby: Raymond Thornton Chandler—the only child of Florence Dart Thornton, an Irish immigrant, and Maurice Benjamin Chandler, a first-generation Irish-American born in Chicago in 1888. Florence and Raymond lived apart from Maurice for long stretches, staying with her sister and brother-in-law in Plattsmouth, Nebraska. Chandler in later years mused about what would have happened if he had grown up in Plattsmouth:

> I would have worked in a hardware store and married the boss's daughter. . . . I might have even got rich—small-time rich, an eight-room house, two cars in the garage, chicken every Sunday, and the *Reader's Digest* on the living-room table, the wife with a cast-iron permanent and me with a brain like a sack of Portland cement.[77]

By Chandler's later account, his father was "found drunk, if at all,"[78] in those early years, and in 1895 Florence weighed her two bad options and decided divorce was better than "drink widow." After the breakup, Maurice dropped away and Chandler neither saw nor heard from him, nor did Maurice send money. His father was there and then he wasn't. Florence, only thirty-five years old, refused to speak her ex-husband's name, denied any culpability for the marriage ending, never worked, and never remarried. It was an absolute break. Florence and Raymond sailed for England.

Now they were the responsibility of Florence's brother, Ernest Thornton. They lived with Florence's mother and a spinster sister in a house in Upper Norwood, near London, that Thornton owned and where Chandler first went to school. The seven-year-old boy was informed that he was "the man of a house" where three grown women lived and that he had rescued his mother from his father.

It was all pretty grim; Chandler was the "boy whose father had gone to the bad."[79] If Chandler was tainted as being his father's son, he adamantly denied the identification and thereby failed the next crucial task. Lacan scholar Richard Klein summarizes Freud:

> In the normal development of the little boy's progress towards heterosexuality, he must pass . . . through the stage of the "positive" Oedipus, a homoerotic identification with his father, a position of effeminized subordination to the father, as a condition of finding a model for his own heterosexual role.[80]

It appears clear that Chandler never did this. Chandler consistently, flatly denied his own alcoholism, a behavior he shared with Maurice Chandler. At age sixty-nine, Chandler was still referring to his father as an "utter swine."[81] In the course of his long and relatively prosperous life, Chandler never tried to find his father.

In 1900 the three women and Chandler moved to Dulwich so that he could attend Dulwich College, the local and respected public school, as a day student, his tuition paid for by Uncle Thornton. In his first year Chandler studied mathematics, music, Latin, French, divinity, and English history. In his second year, he switched to "modern side" courses for "boys who are intended for business." Then, in his third year, he made up the Latin and Greek he had missed the year before and studied "classical side" subjects: Latin, Greek, theology, French, English literature, and Roman history. In his fourth and last year, he was back to taking classes "for boys not proceeding to the university." It is hard to know what was going on: Chandler was nervous, high-strung, and frequently sick[82] and maybe that contributed to the changes in his education's direction, or it may be that Uncle Thornton didn't plan to fund a university education for his nephew.

Chandler was growing up in four doubled, ambiguous states beginning with the question of whether he was an American or an

Englishman—of Irish descent. At home he and his mother were disapproved of because of the divorce, yet the entire household relocated just so he could go to Dulwich College. He hated being under his uncle's thumb, but the man was generous to him. He was being taught at a prestigious school but as a rare day student, making it obvious that Chandler came from a lower class; he would earn the degree but couldn't acquire the pedigree. "His strange and reclusive upbringing," writes Hiney, "was in danger of making him feel odd. . . . In late Victorian England, he was without a clear social class, nationality or male role model."[83] Despite everything, Chandler was consistently first or second in his forms and ever after justifiably proud and respectful of his British public school education.

Chandler left Dulwich at seventeen, and Thornton then paid for a year's study abroad. What Chandler studied appears to have been another compromise between his uncle and himself: German with a tutor in Munich, Nuremberg, and Vienna, preceded by French in a Parisian business school.[84] At the end of his life, he would tell Helga Greene, "The only thing that upset me was the whores at the door of the apartment building if I happened to be out late."[85]

When Chandler came home from the continent, adulthood loomed. As had been made abundantly clear, Uncle Thornton was now through supporting him or his mother. Chandler's grandmother had died, and he and his mother lived together in an apartment. His plan was to find a day job and write poetry at night. He came in third among six hundred candidates on the civil service examination and first in its classics section; he was hired as an assistant store officer, Naval Stores Branch, under the Controller of the Navy. Chafing under a new set of male authority figures, Chandler hated his first job, recalling in a letter forty-four years later: "The idea of being expected to tip my hat to the head of the department struck me as verging on the obscene."[86]

Chandler stuck it out for six months and then, in "an act that enraged his uncle and appalled nearly everybody connected with him,"[87] he quit, left his mother in their apartment, and moved—appropriately for a poet—to a rented room in Bloomsbury. He already had the wardrobe: pinstripe flannel suit, old-school tie and banded straw hat, as well as a cane and gloves.[88] Soon he was back in his mother's apartment but, between 1908 and 1912, he managed to get eight essays, four book reviews, and twenty-seven poems published in reputable magazines. What matters to his later writing was his poetry's "deep strain of romanticism"[89] and its accessibility. Chandler would be proud that he had never subscribed to what he termed the "I-dare-you-not-to-understand-what-I-am-talking-about"[90] school.

For all his passion and scrambling, in the end the money was not there; Chandler couldn't support his mother and himself with his writing in England. Chandler coped in the way he would continue to cope ever more frantically in his future: he moved. He talked his irate uncle into a £500 loan, told his mother he would send for her, and hopped a steamer to New York. Chandler got lucky right away: his best chance at a father figure was already on board.

A man with a remarkably calm demeanor, Warren Lloyd was in the oil business, but his and his wife's enthusiasm was for collecting eclectic, artistic friends. Chandler in his tweeds and aspirations was drawn to them, and they to him. He was invited to look them up if he got as far as Los Angeles.

Chandler worked his way there, running afoul of male authority figures as he did it with, as he would later admit, "a beautiful wardrobe, a public school accent, no practical gifts for earning a living and a contempt for the natives."[91] He got a job in St. Louis but was harassed and called "Lord Stoopentakit," so he moved on to Plattsmouth, Nebraska, and Aunt Grace and Uncle Ernest, a hard-working soul who worked as a boiler inspector. They found their nephew work in a hardware store but things didn't go well with his boss. Thirty-four years later, Chandler would remember: "Since I was fresh out of England at the time and a hardware store was 'trade' I could hardly be expected to get on terms of anything like familiarity with him."[92] Forty-two years later, Chandler didn't like men in charge any better; he was busy checking himself out of psychiatric hospitals and sanitariums against male doctors' orders.

By 1913 he was in the right state but not yet Los Angeles, enduring two southern California–employment indignities: picking apricots and stringing tennis rackets. Then, finally, he wound up on the Lloyds' front stoop. Chandler rented a furnished room but used their home as his mailing address and Warren Lloyd's business connections to get an accounting and bookkeeping job at the Los Angeles Creamery. This position was uncomfortably similar to being the assistant store officer at the Naval Stores Branch. But picking apricots and stringing tennis rackets changes one's perspective.

Maybe it was because Lloyd had secured the creamery job for him that Chandler made clear that he was quickly outstanding in carrying out his duties: "As I knew nothing about accounting, I went to a night school and in six weeks the instructor asked me to leave; he said I had done the three years' course and that was all there was."[93] Years later when Lloyd got him another job, this time in the oil business, Chandler would again inflate his own success.

Beyond the above largesse, Lloyd helped Chandler marry Cissy. The couple had met under his roof. She was then married to the Lloyds' friend, pianist Julian Pascal, and there was a pleasant assumption that Chandler someday would marry the Lloyds' daughter. As it happens, Estelle Lloyd may have been relieved inasmuch as she would later come out as a lesbian. Nevertheless, when Cissy and Chandler announced their love, the Lloyds helped. Their son Paul remembered his parents, Cissy, Julian, Raymond, and Florence all agonizing "over it in an open and civilized way"[94] and the group's eventually deciding that the Pascals should divorce. Later Chandler rewrote the circumstances, claiming that he had rescued Cissy from a bad marriage and gone on to be a model husband.

Chandler could not—or, at least, would not—acknowledge the considerable kindnesses of Warren Lloyd. It appears that Chandler couldn't differentiate between male authority figures who may or may not have treated him as badly as he believed and a father figure with his best interests at heart.

Hammett, Chandler, and Macdonald: three men who won the Oedipal contest with their fathers—dangerous sexual ground in Freud's view. Macdonald, the only hard-boiled writer explicitly to tell Oedipal tales, is saying something more. First, Macdonald makes the experience universal. Second, for a boy to become a man, he actively has to fight his father. Look at sons in Macdonald's novels. In *The Galton Case,* John Galton loses his father through no action of his own, but later he kills Teddy Fredericks, believing him to be his father. *The Chill'*s Alex Kincaid triumphs when he stands up to his father. It takes him two tries. And for the writers: Hammett moved across the country and cut off contact from Richard, and Chandler never looked for Maurice and refused to acknowledge Lloyd's fatherly role. And Macdonald? He turned down Jack's invitation to a last adventure.

What happens next? What happens to sons and mothers?

Chapter Two
Sons and Mothers

While a student at the University of California–Davis, Linda Millar started drinking again. In May 1959 she disappeared into the streets of Stateline, Nevada with two unknown men and later was reported seen in Los Angeles. Ross Macdonald was a reticent man, but he went before television cameras to plead with his daughter to come home. He coordinated a massive search, working with the police in California and Nevada and hiring private detectives who found her in Reno two weeks after she went missing. Linda made an odd, evasive statement about what had happened. By leaving school and drinking, she had violated her ongoing probation, so she was given a suspended sentence for probation violation and the probation was extended. When it was all over, Macdonald collapsed and was hospitalized: severe hypertension with heart damage and kidney stones. His whole family was sick and he felt culpable, convinced that he had "acted as a carrier of neurosis from his own ruined youth to his daughter's."[1]

Macdonald believed what Freud did: that humanity's basic unit is not the individual but the family and that pathologies in families create pathologies in individuals.[2] Fathers in Macdonald's novels

37

tend to harm their sons by leaving them to their mothers; mothers scar their sons by staying too close and using them as husbands. Macdonald's *The Underground Man* features three son/father and two son/father/mother configurations. But the novel's fulcrum is the Snows: a low-IQ, cleft-lipped, man-child, Frederick ("Fritz"), and his unstoppable mother, Edna. She makes uncomfortable hints early on, telling Archer: "I'm afraid you don't understand. Frederick and I are very close"[3] and brightly reminds Fritz, "I'm your girl-friend and you're my boyfriend."[4] Edna has killed three men across two generations—all to deny her damaged son's sexuality. She has isolated him, spoken for him, and thwarted his pitiful attempts to "chase the chicks."[5] The husband/father is dead before the novel starts and is mentioned briefly but memorably: "Mrs. Snow put her fingers to her mouth. A gold wedding band was sunk in the flesh of one finger like a scar."[6] Macdonald also writes, "Her late husband was very much like Fritz."[7] The implication is that Edna treated her husband like a son and her son like a husband. Macdonald is pushing beyond Freud's Oedipus complex: he's positing a mother's damaged longing to be erotically victorious over the other women her son desires, perhaps because it is a way for her to "get back at" a husband by cuckolding him with his son.

It is in *The Chill* that Macdonald looks dead-on at what happens when the incestuous impulses of sons and mothers go wholly un-checked. A close reading of *The Chill*'s last chapter raises the ques-tion: if the son/mother desire is acted upon, what might that look like?

Twenty years passed between Macdonald's mother's death and his daughter's drunken manslaughter and twenty-two years between Tony Galton's disappearance and his son's reappearance in *The Galton Case*: Macdonald is tracing generations. In that same way, *The Chill*'s plot juxtaposes two marriages, one new and the second a generation old, connected by three wrongly solved murders over twenty-two years. In present time Alex Kincaid marries Dolly McGee and the next day she goes missing; Alex hires Archer to find her.

Archer hears that Thomas McGee saw Dolly's wedding picture in the paper, recognized her as the daughter he hadn't seen in ten years, went to the hotel where the couple were staying, talked to Dolly, and disappeared with her.

Ten years earlier, McGee was convicted of murdering his wife. Dolly had found her mother's body and, as a preadolescent, had been pressured into testifying against her father at his trial. Now Dolly is old enough to get married but emotionally stalled exactly at the point where she "won" the Electra-like battle with her mother when the latter was murdered. Still in love with her father, Dolly was then forced to testify against him—effectively killing him. When McGee—who ought to have "given her away" on her wedding— reappears the day after, Dolly chooses her father over her groom, demonstrably stuck in her childhood love.

Dolly is a student at Pacific Point College and works as Dean Roy Bradshaw's mother's driver. Archer learns that Bradshaw is involved with two women: Laura Sutherland, the dean of women, and a newly arrived professor, Helen Haggerty; he has secretly married the former and is being blackmailed by the latter. Helen is murdered; Dolly finds the body, suffers a psychotic break, and is hospitalized. Eventually Archer learns that Bradshaw was having an affair with Dolly's mother at the time of her murder ten years ago.

A third murder, this one twenty-two years earlier, is brought forward. At that time, one of Senator Osborne's daughters, Tish, had an affair with her sister's husband, Luke Deloney. Deloney surprised Tish in bed with a student named Roy Bradshaw. While trying to pistol-whip the two, Deloney was killed when Tish grappled with the gun and it went off. Tish then married Bradshaw, twenty-five years her junior, and paid for his Harvard education. They are living as mother and son in Pacific Point.

It is all too late for Bradshaw: he participated in the cover-up of the Deloney murder twenty-two years ago and again ten years ago when his wife killed Constance McGee. Given that he took no action to stop Tish twice, he is caught for good, a party to murder—and frozen as the adolescent he was twenty-two years ago. So now he sneaks around like a bizarre teenager, manipulating a very sick "mother."

Going into *The Chill*'s final chapter, then, there are two ostensibly grown characters, Dolly Kincaid and Roy Bradshaw, whose maturations were cut off in late childhood as a result of traumatic events beyond their control, and they have suffered or caused suffering ever since.

Archer sees Tish speeding away from her home in her Rolls Royce; she is unable to brake quickly enough to avoid crashing into her son, who is parked in his car in order to block the driveway. Archer observes,

> Old Mrs. Bradshaw had climbed down out of her high protected seat. She seemed unhurt. I remember thinking at that moment that she was an elemental power which nothing could ever kill.
>
> "It's Roy, isn't it? Is he all right?"
>
> "In a sense he is. He wanted out. He's out."
>
> "What do you mean?"
>
> "I'm afraid you've killed him, too."
>
> "But I didn't mean to hurt him. I wouldn't hurt my own son, the child of my womb."
>
> Her voice cracked with maternal grief. I think she half-believed she was his mother, she had lived the role so long. Reality had grown dim.[8]

Bradshaw wanted to stop his mother, but his prudently worn seat belt doesn't save him from Tish's "elemental power" and the fast, slamming force of collision. For her part, Tish has climbed down out of her "high, protected seat" and seems unhurt. In a way, it is her money that has shielded her: money for a bigger, safer car and money that has provided Roy Bradshaw an education. In the larger sense, though, she hasn't ever had the emotional safety she was so bent on. All she has been able to buy was his grudging presence in her bulwarked house. Earlier in *The Chill*, Archer describes that college dean's residence: "The walls of books around me, dense with the past, formed a kind of insulation against the present world and its disasters."[9] As Tish states,

> "I was only protecting my rights. Roy owed me faithfulness at least. I gave him money and background, I sent him to Harvard, I made all his dreams come true."[10]

"Most of his killers are women," Matthew Bruccoli says in *Ross Macdonald*, and "they kill not for love, but for security."[11] Archer continues,

> We both looked down at the dreamless man lying in the road. . . . The jagged lines of blood across his face resembled cracks in a mask through which live tissue showed.[12]

Bradshaw indeed has been leading a masked life. Had he been able to remove it, he would have had a shot at an adult life. Instead, he is dead.

When he writes, "But she had a doubleness in her matching Roy's, and there was element of playacting in her frenzy,"[13] Macdonald is deploying a Freudian trope to advance his fictional purposes.

The psychiatrist in Macdonald's *The Barbarous Coast* asks:

> "Are you familiar with the newer interpersonal theories of psychiatry? With the concept of *folie à deux*? Madness for two, it might be translated. A madness, a violence, may arise out of a relationship even though the parties to the relationship may be individually harmless."[14]

Psychiatrist John Utley explains that folie à deux, now called "shared psychotic disorder" in the *Diagnostic and Statistical Manual of Mental Disorders*, "refers to shared delusion with an unalterable and psychotic state of belief agreed on by two people."[15] It's an apt description of Bradshaw and Tish in *The Chill*: Bradshaw is mentally healthy enough to have succeeded academically and professionally. Had Tish respected the boundaries between mother love and woman/wife love, Bradshaw might have been able to "grow up" sexually. As things stand, Archer tells Tish, "The two of you put on a pretty good act—Godwin [the psychiatrist in *The Chill*] would probably say it fitted both your neurotic needs—but it's over."[16]

Bradshaw's illness may have started as neurosis twenty-two years ago. By the night of his death, he has careened to the other end of a continuum into astounding self-entitlement:

> "And even I deserve something more than I've had. I've lived
> my entire adult life with the consequences of a neurotic in-
> volvement that I got into when I was just a boy."[17]

Roy Bradshaw stands in telling contrast to Alex Kincaid because Bradshaw remains an aging adolescent while Kincaid comes of age. Earlier in *The Chill*, Alex's father shows up and uses the young man's love for his mother to persuade his son to annul his one-day, unconsummated marriage:

> "It's true, isn't it, Alex, you want to come home with me and
> Mother? She's terribly worried about you. Her heart is kick-
> ing up again. . . . I'm only doing what's best for you, son. You
> don't belong with these people. We'll go home and cheer up
> Mother. After all you don't want to drive her into her grave."[18]

The reader is privy almost to the moment when Alex performs the necessary task of a boy's displacement of his erotic desire for his mother onto another, appropriate woman: Alex goes with his father but returns to his wife on his own later the same day. He tells Archer that when he was home with his parents, he felt "as though I wasn't a man any more."[19]

But Bradshaw never completes the displacement; instead, he "loves" an inappropriate woman—inappropriate because she acts as his mother. Tish makes sick, teasing asides early in *The Chill*: "'Roy is a bit of a mother's boy, wouldn't you say?' She looked up at me with complex irony, unembarrassed by his condition or her complicity in it."[20] Later she also contends, "Roy has always been attracted to women who are obviously mammals."[21] Macdonald creates a juvenile Bradshaw who becomes "erotically victorious" with Tish, a woman old enough to be his mother. Here is an example of a young man fixated on his mother—fixation meaning "an arrest of psycho-sexual maturation"[22]—marrying a woman like his mother, thereby "winning" the Oedipal struggle he actually lost as a boy. He then unconsciously recreates his adolescence: his wife calls the shots, and he manipulates her in a mother/son, wife/husband scenario playing out through long years of marriage. For her part, in a flailing attempt at imposed innocence, Tish offloads her sociopathy onto an imaginary, blatantly sexy Letitia Macready:

> She wore very heavy makeup, more appropriate for the stage than the street, and she was hideously overdressed. . . . she had on a leopard-skin—an imitation leopard-skin coat, as I recall, and under it something striped. Sheer hose, with runs in them. Ridiculously high heels. A good deal of costume jewelry. . . . Like a woman of the streets. A greedy, pushing, lustful woman.[23]

There is a lot of sex here: at *The Chill*'s start, Bradshaw is involved with three women. He has had affairs before, as has Tish, who twenty-two years ago bedded her sister's husband and an adolescent student.

For the two of them, sex has been both "just sex" and the driving force behind multiple murders. It ends in tragedy, of course, all around. The clutching, ruined, old woman, "an elemental power which nothing could ever kill," is simply shrieking:

> "I wouldn't hurt my own son, the child of my womb.". . . Her voice cracked with maternal grief. . . . She flung herself on the dead man, as if her old body could somehow warm him back to life and rekindle his love for her. She wheedled and cooed in his ear, calling him a naughty malingering boy for trying to scare her. "Wake up! It's moms."[24]

Freud first identified family romances in 1897, wrote about them in 1908, and published an essay by that name in 1909. Family romances are conscious childhood fantasies fueled by feelings of frustration with faulty parents, rivalry with the parent of the same sex, and competition with siblings. In these romances, the child comforts himself by imagining that he is adopted—that his real parents are of a higher social class, braver, and love him more and exclusively. It is a way of dealing with the inevitable, private disappointments of childhood; Freud calls such daydreams "vents." The romances have at their core the child being erotically victorious. Literature, Freud proposes, works like family romances and neuroses do, consisting "of the imagined, or fantasized, fulfillment of wishes that are either denied by reality or are prohibited by the social standards of morality or propriety."[25]

"Notes of a Son and Father" records four family romances in the Macdonald household: first, Linda was five or six years old when she "couldn't grasp the meaning of what her parents, both full-time writers since the war, were doing alone all day. In search of concrete meaning, she attached herself for awhile to the family of a local postman."[26] Second, the summer she was eleven, Macdonald went back to Ann Arbor to finish writing his dissertation, and "the child expressed a wish to go along and 'keep house' for him."[27] In both of her family romances, Linda's desire to "correct" her "actual life"— to see her wishes fulfilled—is clear.

The third and fourth instances, though, show that in 1956 Macdonald was already puzzling out an extension of Freud's concept. Macdonald and his wife, as parents, also played at family romances: an unmarried aunt who sometimes lived with the Macdonalds and cared for Linda eventually married and had a daughter of her own. Macdonald acknowledges that his and Margaret's "loving treatment of the new child contrasts with their early treatment of their daughter."[28] Then a "neighbor's daughter became almost a foster-daughter of the family especially of the mother"[29]; the girl was, for example, invited along on a family trip to Yosemite several weeks before Linda's catastrophic drunk driving.

> The parents' "foster daughter," the neighbors' daughter, has been perhaps a little too overtly dear to the mother; and this girl is a little prettier in the Hollywood sense, and more sought-after by boys, as well as a "boy-stealer."[30]

Surely her parents' affection for their niece and "foster-daughter" must have felt to Linda like wishes on their part for a better daughter than she was. "The stage was set for a regressive crisis,"[31] Macdonald admits.

In 1964's *The Far Side of the Dollar*, Archer recognizes the unfairness and uselessness of parents and children trying to fulfill each other's wishes.

> I'd just like to change the emphasis slightly. People are trying so hard to live through their children. And the children keep

trying so hard to live up to their parents, or live them down. Everybody's living through or for or against somebody else. It doesn't make too much sense, and it isn't working too well.[32]

Macdonald and his readers saw and knew this: parents believe they are acting out of genuine sacrifice when what is really fueling their behaviors are unexamined wishes.

In Macdonald's *The Instant Enemy*, published in 1968, Bernice Sebastian, the mother of a runaway daughter, eventually recognizes the unfairness of parent-imposed, impossible-to-live-up-to fantasies forced upon a child. "We started a game of let's pretend," she tells Archer, "without ever admitting it to each other."

> Keith was to be the rising young executive and I was to be his model homemaker, making him feel like a man, which is hard for Keith. And Sandy was to make us both feel good by doing well in school and never doing or saying anything wrong. What that boils down to is exploitation. Keith and I were exploiting each other and Sandy, and that's the opposite of loving each other.[33]

Macdonald used the inverse of his relationship with his mother (a mother who becomes a wife, a son who becomes a husband) and exaggerated it when he wrote *The Chill* (a wife who becomes a mother and a husband who becomes a son). Tish's dominance comes from her conscienceless, implacable focus on her husband, who on some level she believes is also her son. Anna ("Annie") Moyer Millar, Ross Macdonald's mother, was fragile and scattered, alternately grasping at her son or railing against him—as though he were her husband. Freud's theory of anxiety applies:

> Anxiety is the response to helplessness in the face of danger. If the danger has struck, the anxiety is automatic and immediate.

If the danger is still in the offing, anxiety is the *anticipation* of helplessness in the face of danger. The overwhelming preponderance of anxiety falls into the category of anticipation.[34]

Annie must have felt helpless while waiting for Macdonald's birth: she had had three late-term miscarriages, was forty years old, and in a shaky marriage with Jack Millar. She and Jack fought, Macdonald later said, "about the things that poor people argue about."[35] It was the beginning of Macdonald's lifelong worry about having enough money. By forty-five, Annie looked like an old woman and her married life in California was effectively over, although there would be widely spaced and brief reconciliations and never a divorce. She and her son were back living in her native, cold Canada with her dour Mennonite mother and sister. Annie was childlike, seeing reality in absolute ways: they were indeed poor, but she did not need to sell homemade dusting cloths door to door or beg for food on the street with her uneasy little boy at her side. There was a falling out at the house that Macdonald didn't understand, and he and his mother had to move out. He felt guilty in the face of circumstances he could not possibly have been responsible for, much less controlled: his father's leaving, his and his mother's ouster from his grandmother's house, and his mother's hysteria.

Then Annie gave way altogether: "she brought the six-year-old to an orphanage and filled out papers to have him admitted," Macdonald remembered. "The iron gates of the orphanage were branded in his memory like the gates to the Mennonites' hell."[36] At the last moment Macdonald's sobs weakened Annie's resolve. She didn't know Rob Millar at all, a cousin of her husband's who stepped in and took the boy. Macdonald had been given proof: the world was dangerous, and he could not trust his mother to protect him.

When Macdonald was sixteen, he made a count: he had lived in more than fifty houses "and committed the sin of poverty in every one of them."[37] He shuttled between relatives with interim stays with his mother in rooming houses, where they shared a bed "far past a proper age." Annie "was devoted to him in ways that seemed unhealthy."[38] Certainly Macdonald was afraid of his mother. Annie couldn't check her own impulses in her relationship with her son. A boy who desires his mother but senses that this is proscribed is reassured by a mother who can be trusted. But in the case of a mother who might do anything, that's free-fall territory. And so Macdonald alternately fled from Annie and tried to "manage" her. In "Notes of a Son and Father," Macdonald describes her and himself:

> Her devotion to this child was hysterically intense; periodic hysteria was the keynote of her last twenty years. Her relationship to her son swung between passionate love and violent upbraiding. He came to know her weaknesses very young, and tempered the wind to her as much as he could, loving and hating her.[39]

"He's very good at deceiving people," Archer says of Roy Bradshaw in *The Chill*, "living on several levels, maybe deceiving himself to a certain extent. Mother's boys get that way sometimes."[40]

"Mother's boys" are the unfortunate norm. The template for ancient Greek families in myth was still there, in play, in how Macdonald experienced his childhood and in how he structured his later fiction. As Phillip Slater puts it, ancient family systems "intensify the mother-son relationship at the expense of the husband-wife relationship."[41] Mid-twentieth-century Western cultural patterns lent lip service to that husband-wife connection but gave mothers little support, especially when there was no extended family nearby and no work outside the home.

Both family systems tend to produce male children who are highly Oedipal. The systems are alike in depriving women of contact with and participation in the total culture, and in creating a domestic pattern peculiarly confining and unfulfilling. They thus encourage a vicarious involvement of the mother in the life of the son. Both systems, furthermore, place an emotional overload on the mother-son relationship: the Greek system by forcing the mother to put the son in the father's place, the American by making child rearing a fulltime occupation and removing the child in its earliest years from other socializing agents.[42]

"My mother was without resources,"[43] Macdonald told an interviewer many years later. It was a sadly true summation of Annie's life. She was an utterly unfit mother, but it was hellish being her too. "It was a bad night for mothers," says Archer in *The Underground Man*. "And a bad night for sons."[44]

"My mind had been haunted for years by an imaginary boy whom I recognized as the darker side of my own remembered boyhood," writes Macdonald about *The Galton Case*. "I couldn't think of him without anger and guilt."[45] In his sixteen years, Macdonald's anxiety had been manifest in myriad behaviors: bullying, theft, fighting, early drinking, and the repeated physical seduction of a mentally retarded maid. He was shamed by what he did, making no connection between his overt behavior and its underlying sources.

Kreyling delineates those sources in psychoanalytic terms:

Freudian theory, of course, is dominated by sex; our development of consciousness is not possible without the somatic, or bodily, development of sexualized anatomies, the realization of desires that grow with them, and the guilt that inevitably comes with learning the rules. Nor do we develop in isolation; for better or worse we develop in families.[46]

Over and over again in Macdonald's fiction, the killers are parents who consciously or not use a child's sad confusion over knowing-without-knowing that he sexually desires that parent. As a boy, Macdonald was both aware of societal taboos and absent patterning from his parents. Taboos—including the one against incest—are the stuff of rigid self-discipline; and Macdonald's rules for himself—no fighting, stealing, sexual bullying, or homosexuality—are not so different from Hammett's of no fighting, driving, shooting and, later, sex.

Sometime in his late adolescence there was an endpoint to Macdonald's criminality: he did some last wrong thing, and whoever caught him made Macdonald run while tied to a moving car. After that, for whatever combination of reasons, he was able to forgo criminal behaviors. Macdonald biographer Tom Nolan stresses how much this self-mastery mattered to Macdonald, who

> dealt with the worst impulses of his own personality—rage, self-pity, the urge to do harm—by suppressing them. He'd keep himself under rigid control. This was as serious to him as life or death, for he knew he had the strength and anger to kill. Thoughts of succumbing to evil terrified him.[47]

This was the beginning of a remarkably "successful" willed performance on Macdonald's part. It lasted for one generation of Macdonald's family.

In 1932 Jack Millar died, leaving a life insurance policy payable to Annie, who gave it to Macdonald, which enabled him to enroll in college. During his sophomore year at the University of Western Ontario, "the boy was strong enough and had 'forgiven enough'" to invite his mother, who "was gradually breaking up," to live with him. He came home one day in December 1935 to find her naked and helpless; she died of a brain tumor before Christmas. Fifteen

years and some fifty houses after those iron gates, Macdonald was
now an actual orphan.

Macdonald's fear of failure was a fear of the failure to love his
father, mother, and daughter enough:

> [His father was] visited by the son, who was ashamed of him
> and also loved him, but not enough. . . . [I]n her last days as
> she lay dying of a brain tumor, he loved her as one loves a
> child, but failed to love her enough. . . . [T]he baby [Linda]
> was very beautiful and bright, but her parents could not love
> her enough. [48]

What would "enough" have looked like? Would it have been the
ability on Macdonald's part to make his father, mother, and daughter
"okay"? That inability, that "not loving enough," engendered misplaced guilt. And because the guilt was misplaced, it couldn't be
resolved. Moreover, with the death of his parents, he lost any opportunity to go back and, this time, do the right thing and "love them
enough." So, he did what he could do now that Jack and Annie were
dead; he turned his back on his past and fully reinvented himself.

But when his adolescent daughter fell apart in terrible ways,
Macdonald realized that his refusal to look at his own childhood
had stunted his daughter's. It all felt too late: as Helen Haggerty
cries in *The Chill*, "Everything important—it was all over before I
knew it had started."[49] First, Macdonald couldn't start all over, so of
course his willed performance hadn't worked: twenty-two years after
his mother's death, Macdonald still felt guilty when he was writing
"Notes of a Son and Father":

> He blames himself still for spending too little time with her
> on her deathbed, and when the time came ignorantly allowing
> her to die without his presence. Perhaps it was his twenty-

year-old revenge on her for her failure to make a marriage
and a home. Anyhow, the fact and circumstances of her death
remain among his recurrent and most monumental images,
sleeping and waking.[50]

Second, in turning his back on his mother, he cut himself off from
future intimacy with other women. Therapist Terrence Real, who
writes about male depression, argues against such disconnection in
"The Loss of the Relational":

> [T]he true meaning of psychological "separation" is maturity,
> and we humans stand a better chance of maturing when we
> do not disconnect from one another. . . . what maturity truly
> requires is the replacement of childish forms of closeness
> *with more adult forms of closeness*, not with dislocation.
>
> As devastating as the disconnection from the mother may
> be, it is merely the beachhead of a larger social mandate, the
> instruction to turn away, not just from the mother but from
> intimacy itself.[51]

What Macdonald is arguing in his best fiction extends psychoanalytic thinking: Macdonald believes disconnection is not only ill
advised but impossible. Psychoanalysis, classic myths, and fiction:
all are about the connections among family members. Novels are
really identity quests, exercises in connection-realization, organized
by archetypes-in-common in the minds of writers, characters, and
readers. In her essay, "Finding the Connections," published after
Macdonald's death, Eudora Welty analyzes how his novels work:

> Where, and from how long ago, out of what human fissure,
> did this crime start, and why at this moment did it erupt?
> What connections will lead us back to the source? The iden-
> tity of the man or woman there to be found can be reached

only through following this network of connections. It's the connections that absorb the author and magnetize his plots into their intricate and daunting patterns.[52]

Macdonald describes his detective this way:

> His actions are largely directed to putting together the stories of other peoples' lives and discovering their significance. He is less a doer than a questioner, a consciousness in which the meanings of other lives emerge.[53]

Thus Macdonald straightforwardly chose to be an identity-quest novelist, and he redesigned Archer to suit that purpose. The journey in each Macdonald novel is Archer's coming to understand, sympathize with, and forgive the connections among the other characters. Moreover, Macdonald's readers participate in that adventure; they are on identity-quests of their own, seeing themselves not in Archer, who is only the explainer, but in the other characters.

Hammett and Chandler were unintentional self-realizing writers, and their detectives share their unease with human connections. The posed question in Hammett and Chandler's work is: can the detectives do the jobs at hand without compromising their personal code—that is, without getting close enough to other people to be changed by them? Readers hoping to be changed by the experience of reading a Hammett or Chandler novel have to puzzle out the connections and meanings because nobody's forthcoming: not the authors and not their alter egos. Connections and concomitant meanings are there, but they are harder to find, hidden by Hammett and downright lied about by Chandler.

The Smart Set published Hammett's first fiction in its October 1922 issue. "The Parthian Shot" is about Paulette Key, who realizes that her six-month-old son is as stupid and obstinate as her irritating husband. So Paulette gets the baby christened "Don," sends him home from the church with the baby nurse, and then boards a train heading west. The clever part, of course, is that the child's name is now "Don Key." The iconoclastic Hammett probably appreciated the guts it took for a mother to light out for the territory. He and Jose, living with a baby in a tiny apartment, would have known how thrilling what Paulette did was. But it is hard to read much meaning into a 100-word, flippant story for which Hammett was paid $1.13.

A dozen years later, Hammett invented a mother for *The Thin Man*: Mimi Wynant beats her nearly grown children, who are terrified of her; reflexively lies; and has collaborated for money with her ex-husband's murderer. As he does with the other deadly females in his canon, Hammett describes Mimi's psychopathic rage in inhuman terms:

> Mimi made an animal noise in her throat, muscles thickened on the back of her neck. . . . Mimi's face was becoming purple. Her eyes protruded, glassy, senseless, enormous. Saliva-bubbled and hissed between clenched teeth with her breathing, and her red throat—her whole body—was a squirming mass of veins and muscles swollen until it seemed they must burst. Her wrists were hot in my hand and sweat made them hard to hold.[54]

It sounds like penile arousal, yet it is a description of a woman. The obvious reference is to the "phallic mother"—one of Freud's stages in a little boy's development wherein he assumes his mother has a penis; and when he finds that she does not, he is horrified and begins fearing his own castration. Did Hammett study Freud? They shared Blanche Knopf as their editor. Was he consciously aping

Freud in *The Thin Man*? It almost doesn't matter: what is telling is that when Hammett wanted to describe a very scary woman, he unconsciously knew that a phallic mother would be terrifying.

There is a famous sexual reference to the above scene in *The Thin Man*: Nora afterward asks her husband, "Tell me something, Nick. Tell me the truth: when you were wrestling with Mimi, didn't you get excited?"[55] "The *New York Times* carried an ad reading, 'I don't believe the question on page 192 of Dashiell Hammett's *The Thin Man* has had the slightest influence upon the sale of the book,' followed by Alfred A. Knopf's signature."[56] Hammett biographer and Englishman Julian Symons later wrote: "The question was omitted from the English edition. Erections did not exist in English fiction at that time."[57] Humor aside, it is revealing that Nick Charles is asked about arousal from a physical fight with an angry, out-of-control mother and admits, "Oh, a little," to which his wife laughs and says, "If you aren't a disgusting old lecher."[58]

In the twelve years between "The Parthian Shot" and *The Thin Man*, there are no mothers in Hammett's fiction. It is striking, really, and particularly so for an author who first and steadily loved his mother, and thereafter found three mother figures.

His full name was Samuel Dashiell Hammett, but it was the "Dashiell" that mattered; it was his mother Anne's maiden name. Which came first: Anne's belief that the Hammetts were inferior to the Dashiells or her husband's failure to keep jobs and marriage vows? In either event, Annie told her son, "All men are no good."

> Then she added, if you couldn't keep your husband with love, do it with sex. She told him that a woman who wasn't good in the kitchen wouldn't be much good in any of the other rooms either, words he would remember all his life.[59]

It is hard to know how to take this: Anne clearly thought that her male child Dashiell was "good" and she wasn't able to "keep" her husband faithful via love, sex, or cooking. Moreover, after he left Jose, Hammett espoused neither domesticity nor monogamy ever again. In any event, all his life Hammett was closer to his mother than his father. Partly it was appreciation and admiration: Anne, more than Richard, was the hardworking, reliable parent, despite her tuberculosis and the status of women. Hammett was scrawny and whip smart, a quirky little kid only a mother could love, and Anne did; she championed him.

Although there are few mothers in Hammett's fiction, there are plenty of tough, disillusioned wives with weak, disappointing husbands—especially in his stories. Hammett used Anne as a wife early in his career, but didn't transfer her as a mother. Here is LeRoy Lad Panek in *Reading Early Hammett: A Critical Study of the Fiction Prior to* The Maltese Falcon: "He started out with a caustic look at marriage and 'The Parthian Shot' skewer[s] the ways that women and men undermine the institution."[60] Eloise, in "The Joke on Eloise Morey," is a large woman looming over her puny husband. She's a hammerer:

> You were a genius; you were going to be famous and wealthy and God knows what all! And I fell for it and married you: a milk-and-water nincompoop who'll never amount to anything. . . . Delicate! Weak and wishy-wash.[61]

Her husband—appropriately called Dudley—slinks away and kills himself, leaving a final, groveling love letter to Eloise as his suicide note. Unnerved by the note, Eloise destroys it and is thereby undone. Neighbors volunteer recollections of Eloise wishing her husband were dead, and she's arrested as his murderer—which she is, in some sense.

Margaret, in "The Ruffian's Wife," is identified in terms of her husband, Guy (another apt name), and she begins by seeing him as a larger-than-life, romantic outlaw.

What, she wondered with smug assurance that it never could have happened to her, would it be like to have for a husband a tame, housebroken male who came regularly to meals and bed, whose wildest flying could attain no giddier height than an occasional game of cards, a suburbanite's holiday in San Francisco, or, at the very most, a dreary adventure with some stray stenographer, manicurist, milliner?[62]

However, when the Bolivian pearl concessionaire who lent Guy money for his latest failed scheme shows up, Margaret's view of her husband shrinks to realistic proportions. He is just a guy who needs her help. She does help him murder the Bolivian, but the marriage is over: "The plain truth was she had never seen Guy as a man, but always as a half-fabulous being. The weakness of any defense she could contrive for him lay in his needing a defense."[63] It is a recurring progression in what Hammett called his "sex stories": the bride adores her groom because she inaccurately and unfairly sees him as invincible, only to turn on him when he proves vulnerable. In the long, angry battle thereafter, the wife is the tougher combatant; in *Red Harvest*, there are "men with the dull look of respectable husbands."[64] Marriage is the big cheat. This all looks like Hammett's parents' marriage rather than his own, and it introduces the larger issue of men needing help.

Nevertheless, Anne and Richard were emotionally healthy enough to raise a son able to make his way, however imperfectly and incompletely, through Freud's developmental steps; and this successful journey rendered Hammett open to mother and father figures too. When Hammett was the father, he gave his daughters permission to conjure family romances of their own, and Jo later wrote about it:

Once when I was ten or eleven, he accused me of being ashamed of my parents. Then not waiting for an answer, he went on to say that it was okay; everyone was ashamed of his parents. When he was little, he said, he liked to imagine that he was adopted, and one stormy night his "real" father would come driving down the road to reclaim him. He didn't go on to explain what this "real" father would be like, but I imagined he would be very different from the one he already had.[65]

When Hammett sent the manuscript for "Poisonville" to Alfred A. Knopf in February 1928, it was Blanche Knopf who wrote back: "There is no question whatever that we are keen about the ms. . . . Hoping that we will be able to get together on POISONVILLE (a hopeless title by the way)."[66] Hammett's reply was:

> Somehow I had got the idea that "Poisonville" was a pretty good title and I was surprised at your considering it hopeless— sufficiently surprised to ask a couple of retail book sellers what they thought of it. They agreed with you, so I'm beginning to suspect which one of us is wrong.[67]

Knopf published Hammett's first novel as *Red Harvest* one year later. Blanche became his editor, thus moving the pulp-writing Hammett into heavyweight company; in addition to Freud, she also edited Gide, de Beauvoir, Camus, Van Vechten, and Cather. Blanche was one kind of mother to Hammett: a steady taskmaster, hard charging and without subterfuge.

Rose Evans was Hammett's motherly housekeeper and meddler. Hammett biographer Diane Johnson paraphrased what Evans said in an interview after her boss's death:

> Women came around, tried to get money out of him; Rose tried her best to keep them away, but they came around at night too when Rose had gone home. She didn't know what

went on when she wasn't there. Gold diggers. She knew what they were.[68]

When Hammett was about to be released from prison (having run afoul of the U.S. District Court of the Southern District of New York), Rose sent him two suits, two shirts, and two pairs of shoes, "so he'd have a choice."[69] She was there when he was dying, and Hammett scholar Richard Layman subsequently learned that Lillian Hellman "wanted to hire Rose Evans, but Hammett asked her not to take the job because he feared she would not be treated with the respect and affection which he had always felt for her."[70]

When Hammett was convicted of contempt of court for refusing to answer questions about the Bail Fund Committee of the Civil Rights Congress of New York, bail was set at $10,000. Hellman later claimed that she tried and failed to raise the money, but it was steady, loyal Muriel Alexander who showed up with $10,000 cash. It did no good: "You couldn't get bail from just anywhere, you had to say where it came from and the court had to like where it came from."[71] The court decided there was something fishy about a sec-retary coming up with $10,000 and therefore refused Hammett bail. Fifty-eight years later, Hammett's granddaughter was emotional and emphatic: "That woman went to her grave without ever revealing where she got the money!"[72]

As the years played out, Jose became a kind of mother figure for Hammett. She was, after all, a nurse like his mother. Jo remembered:

Papa would come and stay with us sometimes in the thirties—when he was drinking and things were not going well with him. Our house was a refuge from his other worlds. My mother cooked and tended to him, tried to get him to eat.[73]

When Hammett was in prison, Jose worried.

I think Mother understood better than I did how hard prison would be on him. . . . And she was less deceived by the tough-guy front he always wore. She knew his physical frailty, had nursed him in the San Francisco days when they both thought he was dying. She knew how much he needed his privacy and understood what its loss would mean to him.[74]

For his part, Hammett tended to tease his mother figures affectionately, including Jose in later years, treating them like kid sisters— which may have been how he treated his mother too. The man who bloomed in male institutions certainly knew how to charm women. Jo marveled at his finesse:

The servants loved him. "Mr. Hammett never asks for anything special," they said. He didn't have to. Somehow people were always trying to please him, to give him what he wanted before he asked for it. I'd noticed that before. It was some sort of trick he'd learned. Though I saw that it worked for him, I could never figure out how he did it.[75]

Chandler never got to Hammett's kind of ease. Doubleness led to loneliness in Chandler's writing and life, and most of that loneliness had to do with women, gay men, and sex. Chandler was unable—or at least unwilling—to draw nuanced female characters, much less complicated male/female relationships. This proved a weakness as his work moved from short stories to novels, and from genre to mainstream. It was a startling deficiency in otherwise thoughtful and beautiful work. Nevertheless, there is much to be learned by watching that failing play out.

Chandler's novels have double geographies; the "outer one" is crucially set in Los Angeles. Chandler was masterful and confident in this outer diegesis, with its poetry of place and empathetic characterizations. Nonetheless, he uncomfortably—and perhaps unconsciously—knew that this was not where the fundamental crime's motivations came from, nor where its solution could be understood. Chandler scholar Stephen Knight writes:

> Essentially the novels have double plots. There is an outer structure where what has gone wrong is loosely associated with corruption, gangsters, professional crime. . . . But none of these people or patterns turns out really to have been behind the central crime, and they fade from the action as the inner, personalized plot is steadily revealed, as the actual betrayer and killer becomes exposed.[76]

These inner narratives reveal their author. "The whole pattern is common in the novels," says Knight. "The villain is consistently a sexy woman who gets very close to the hero."[77] And the hero—the detective/first-person narrator/Marlowe—is very close to Chandler. The great puzzle in Chandler is that he made Marlowe "a shop-soiled Galahad" who rescues women all over Los Angeles, yet the women are fiends. Marlowe acknowledges in *The Big Sleep* that the "move with the knight was wrong. . . . Knights had no meaning in this game. It wasn't a game for knights."[78]

Chandler's illogical formula is, in fact, fully compatible with Hammett's espoused conundrum. One of the genre's descriptors is that the detective never wins: he never gets rich, never makes his mark, and never gets the girl. Richard Layman elaborates:

> The burden of the tragedy was borne by the detective, who typically narrated the tale, acting as both chorus and hero.

Physically, he was invulnerable; spiritually, though, he was jaded by the awesome knowledge that his job, which was to bring order to a chaotic world, could never be completed. He was a seedy Sisyphus afflicted with an unrealizable moral vision.[79]

Hammett and Chandler's narrating heroes simultaneously believe in the power of self-determination and despair that the self had no power in the world. This can function as their definition of hard-boiled fiction: an existential man in a nihilistic world.

In Chandler's *The High Window*, Jasper Murdock had made advances on Merle Davis, his wife's neurotic little assistant. Then he was murdered—defenestrated. With his death, a rare category of Chandler monster is created: the widowed mother. "[T]he female threatens the male," wrote Knight about *The High Window*, "as a bogus mother rather than a bogus lover."[80] Elizabeth Murdock plays her regrettable son, Leslie, and, acting as a mother figure, overruns her assistant, Merle, then hates them both for their weakness. Elizabeth has rendered her son superficial: his wife has given up and left him, and he gambles extravagantly. Elizabeth tells Marlowe, "I have a damn fool of a son. . . . he is quite incapable of earning a living and he has no money except what I give him, and I am not generous with money. . . . I find him dull myself."[81] Elizabeth is masterful at using the psychological advantages that accrue to a mother: with time and cunning, and without conscience, Elizabeth has convinced Merle that she pushed Mr. Murdock out the window, that she owes her continued job to the forgiveness of her mistress, and that her mistress is so emotionally fragile that she must never be confronted with painful truths. Marlowe shows Merle a photograph of Elizabeth killing her husband and then tells Merle:

You were made to think you had pushed him. It was done with care, deliberation and the sort of quiet ruthlessness you only find in a certain kind of woman dealing with another woman. . . . She had the strange wild possessive love for her son such women have. She's cold, bitter, unscrupulous and she used you without mercy or pity. . . . You were just a scapegoat to her. If you want to come out of this pallid sub-emotional life you have been living, you have got to realize and believe what I am telling you.[82]

And Merle's response? She tells Marlowe, "You must never show this to Mrs. Murdock. It would upset her terribly."[83]

There are sad pieces of Chandler in the novel's victims. Leslie, the cowed son, "a slim, tall, self-satisfied-looking number," is similar to the Chandler who showed up at the Lloyds' Friday evening get-togethers, "an elegant young thing trying to be brilliant about nothing,"[84] by his own description. And then there is Merle, with her "pallid sub-emotional life," overstimulated in the company of any man. She is Chandler-like too. "When it came to women, [Chandler] was highly excitable," Chandler biographer Judith Freeman describes. "He was drawn to their beauty, but they made him nervous, overly anxious to please; they caused such an excess of emotion, an intense response."[85]

Macdonald, Hammett, and Chandler: of the three, Chandler's childhood was the least amenable to his playing family romances. His mother had implacably appropriated the fantasist role: in her eyes and therefore in her powerless son's, she was "a sort of saint," and his father was "an utter swine." It's a cruel irony that, of the three, the young aspiring writer most needing a father figure was also the least equipped to recognize one.

When Chandler met Cissy Pascal at the Lloyds' one Friday night in 1913, she was overtly different from his mother, Florence. Cissy was divorced and remarried, had lived in New York City, where she had posed nude—maybe for a painting over a bar—and may have smoked opium. She was a showy redhead and game for anything. He got the idea that he couldn't fail her. Hiney thinks that Chandler saw Cissy as

> without the fragility he was wary of in women. Her colorful past had given Cissy both a cynicism towards convention and an independent spirit. Having married twice, she had a wit and resourcefulness that Florence Thornton had never quite managed in the face of bad luck. Cissy was a worldly and beautiful woman whom Chandler could talk to on equal terms without worrying that her feelings might be easily hurt, or that she would be in need of constant reassurance.[86]

Freeman agrees: Cissy had none "of the vulnerability and sadness of his mother—the fragility of an abandoned woman. In her life, it was Cissy who'd done the abandoning, not the other way around."[87]

By 1916 Florence Chandler's son had sent for her. She fit right in with the Lloyds and all their friends, especially Julian and Cissy Pascal. There is an incongruous set of photographs: in one of mother and son together on the beach, she is tentative and a little grim, in a buttoned-up wool coat and hose; and he is in a wool suit and vest, smoking a pipe. In another beach shot—this time his mother isn't there—Chandler is grinning, lounging in a bathing suit, sporting a tan. Chandler is fully two people: one with his mother and another without her.

Chandler was twenty-eight, living with his mother, and queasily in love with a married woman. Life got uncomfortably down to the nub, so Chandler moved. He and Gordon Pascal (Julian's son and Cissy's stepson) joined the Canadian army. Florence moved in with Julian and Cissy for the duration. By March 1918 Chandler had been trained as an infantryman and was suddenly on the front lines in France. Casualties mounted fast and Chandler found himself a stunned platoon leader way too soon. It took him thirty-nine years to write about what happened next, and then he did so in just two brief letters to a young Australian correspondent whom he had never met.

> If you had to go over the top somehow all you seemed to think of was trying to keep the men spaced, in order to reduce casualties. It was always very difficult, especially if you had replacements or men who had been wounded. It's only human to want to bunch for companionship in face of heavy fire.[88]

In June 1918, German artillery shells blew up his entire outfit: every man died except Chandler; he had suffered a concussion and was removed from the front. He had enlisted just ten months before. "I have lived my whole life on the edge of nothing," he wrote. "Once you have had to lead a platoon into direct machine-gun fire, nothing is ever the same again."[89]

Chandler wrote an unfinished, unpublished sketch about that last bombardment called "Trench Raid," and he transposed that same terrible attack into a fleeting aside about the World War II experience of Terry Lennox in *The Long Goodbye*, his late and most autobiographical novel. Otherwise, Chandler never spoke of what had happened to him in France. The war increased Chandler's tendency toward detachment. The subterfuges were there before the wartime slaughters, and the slaughters only strengthened the subterfuges. Marlowe would affect that same stance: "It all depends on where you sit and what your own private score is," Marlowe says in *The Long Goodbye*. "I didn't have one. I didn't care. I finished the drink and went to bed."[90] They both did care.

When Chandler came home from the war, he found his mother sick with cancer and spending increasing hours in her bedroom at the Pascals. A poem that he wrote then, "Lines With an Incense Burner," includes the stanzas "The secret and silence and perfume . . . in the quiet house of all the dead."[91]

Cissy and Chandler wanted to marry, but Florence couldn't be appeased and Chandler wouldn't cross her. There was no way around it; he and Cissy would have to wait until Florence died. They would wait four years. Chandler supported two women in two Los Angeles apartments, and he lived with his mother until she died at the end of January 1924.

Chandler's mother chose her response to her husband's neglect: she handed over the responsibility for her own life to her son. Of course, this was what women alone often did at that time: divorce was a hard stigma then, and she was frightened. The fact that she made the expected moves doesn't contradict the truth that her decision damaged her son. In a real sense, she used him.

Without doubt, Chandler saw his mother as the innocent victim and himself as having wanted to rescue her. At sixty-nine he still unreservedly adored her: "I knew that my mother had affairs—she was a very beautiful woman—and the only thing I felt to be wrong was that she refused to marry again for fear a step-father would not treat me kindly."[92]

Psychologist John D. Gartner explains the tyranny of what Freud terms the "repetition compulsion":

> Put simply, there is a powerful *unconscious* drive to recreate in one's adult relationships the relationships you experienced as a child. In my twenty years of practicing psychotherapy, there is no single idea that I have found to be more useful or universal. . . . It is as if, when we are born, our minds are like wet plaster, and the structure of the relationships we encounter forms an impression that hardens into a mold. . . . What feels right to us, powerfully and compellingly so, are the comfortable and familiar relational patterns of the past.[93]

Certainly Chandler would frequently misread women, in just such terms. It was as if he saw women in broad categories, as tropes.

Given that he had experienced Florence as ostensibly fragile and a "sort of saint," Chandler would spend a lifetime hell-bent on saving complicated women. And Philip Marlowe did so too; Chandler could not write what he could not understand. Yet Chandler, at some subconscious level, did understand more about his mother, that "more" becoming apparent in his invented female monsters. As Freeman puts it:

> Ray's own mother bullied him, forcing him to wait until she was dead before he could marry Cissy. He never could say anything bad about his mother, certainly not while she was alive, but in his . . . fictional portraits of women—especially older women—what often leaks through is loathing, resentment, revulsion and fear.[94]

It all made Marlowe and Chandler lonely for and frightened of women. Jerry Speir, who also writes about Macdonald, agrees:

> Chandler was strongly affected by and often mistaken about women at various periods throughout his life. . . . Part of the impulse was to protect women, honor them, put them on a pedestal in the manner of the chivalric knight; the other impulse was to separate himself from them lest he be somehow contaminated by a foreignness which he has only vague reasons for fearing.[95]

In Freud's version, family romances are the purview of the powerless child's. The fantasies provide a "vent" to ease the disappointment of having inevitably imperfect parents. As such, fantasies alleviate a little the "bone of my bone" bond between parent and child; family romances are a healthy, necessary stage in a child's maturation. In Macdonald's retooled family romances, however, it is the adults who are conjuring perfect children; it is the all-powerful parents imposing their own fantasies on their inescapably disappointing sons and daughters. In Macdonald's finest novels, "playing happy families" is a deadly game ending in scarred children. Macdonald is writing cautionary tales that ring true, echoing something that readers already, consciously or unconsciously, knew: parents really do impose their unrealistic fantasies on the weakest members of their family—which is to say, they don't always see, much less celebrate, the actual child.

Chapter Three

Sons and Lovers

There are tipping points in marriages, often not recognized as such until much later. When Linda Millar was being held for manslaughter, her mother, Margaret Millar, told District Attorney Vern Thomas that she had never discussed the accident with her daughter. Moreover, she said, "I have never been present when Linda discussed the accident with anyone. . . . Her father took over all that. They were trying to—he has always spared me things, because I get upset."[1] Fifteen years later and like her paternal grandfather, Linda died young of a stroke at thirty-one. Macdonald wrote to a friend that "she was a valiant girl, one of the great moral forces in my life," and to another, "The people who knew her best, including her husband and me, felt that she was in almost unaccountable ways a great person."[2] The absence of references to what Margaret thought is striking. Somewhere in a long and frequently angry marriage complicated by an iron-willed daughter, Margaret had run through her emotional stores. How much of a marriage was left?

James Pagnusat, the seven-year-old son Linda left behind, spent nearly every weekend at the Millars' house for many months after his mother's death. Macdonald was desperate to protect the boy and

particularly to safeguard him from his mother's problems. Peter
Wolfe, who would go on to write books about Hammett, Chandler,
and Macdonald, was visiting Macdonald at that time and was struck
by how fiercely Macdonald "*loved* that boy."[3] He taught him to swim,
and the two read to each other. And he wrote his grandson into *The
Underground Man* as Ronny Broadhurst.

That *The Underground Man* was reviewed on the front page of the
New York Times Book Review and by Eudora Welty was a landmark.
The Underground Man would be Macdonald's most successful novel.
Welty correctly sees that

> what really concerns Archer, and the real kernel of the book,
> its heart and soul, is the little boy of six, good and brave and
> smart. He constitutes the book's emergency. . . . Ronny is the
> tender embodiment of everything Archer is by nature bound
> to protect, infinitely worthy of rescue.[4]

In the novel, Archer doesn't even look for the killer until after three
children, including Ronny, are found and safely home. Welty knows
that, in Macdonald,

> the mystery and its solution are twin constructions in his hands,
> based on the same secret, which is always one of serious human
> import. This secret is often buried in a family's past, and it
> needs to be made known *now*—urgently, in order to save a
> life, often a child's or a young person's.[5]

It is curious to look at whom Archer considers children in need
of loving protection. In addition to six-year-old Ronny, the two other
"young people [who] had slipped away over the curve of the world"[6]
are adolescents. In the novel's last pages, Archer goes back to rescue
a fourth, Fritz, grown but retarded and playing husband to another
angry mother. Archer's presence in the Snow family dynamites it.

Peter Wolfe likens what happens to Oedipus: "Like the ruinous last interview between Oedipus and his mother, Jocasta, the mother/son encounter rending the novel has the drive of tragedy."[7] Although a damaged Oedipus, Fritz stands his mother down, and that is his triumph.

Fritz had bought a wig, beard, and mustache from a movie magazine and tells Archer:

> "I wanted to chase the chicks on Sunset Strip. And be a swinger."
>
> "Did you catch any?"
>
> He shook his doleful head. "I only got to go the once. She doesn't want me to have a girlfriend."
>
> His gaze moved past me to his mother. . . .
>
> I turned to her. "Let him do his own talking, please."
>
> The sharpness in my voice seemed to encourage her son: "Yeah.
>
> Let me do my own talking. . . . What happened to my wig and stuff?"
>
> "Somebody must have taken it," she said.
>
> "I don't believe that. I think you took it," he said.
>
> "That's crazy talk."
>
> His eyes came up to her face, slowly, like snails ascending a wall. "You swiped it from under the mattress." He struck the bed under him with his hand to emphasize the point. "And I'm not crazy."
>
> "You're talking that way," she said. "What reason would I have to take your wig?"
>
> "Because you didn't want me to chase the chicks. You were jealous."[8]

The sexual dynamic between Roy and Tish Bradshaw in *The Chill* is ruinous, but at least it is a bargain between two people who are otherwise functioning as adults. Here, in *The Underground Man*, Edna is exploiting her innocent, undeserving son.

The Underground Man has another mother, more well meaning but nevertheless unwittingly stunting her son's maturity too. Years before the novel begins, Leo Broadhurst had an affair with an adolescent girl, left his wife, Elizabeth, and disappeared, seemingly forever. Their eleven-year-old son, Stanley, was left to his mother. Edna Snow tells Archer, "Poor little Stanley was sick and shaking. . . . he couldn't help hearing the quarrel, and he was old enough to know what it meant. He ran out and tried to stop his father, but Captain Broadhurst roared away."[9]

Archer says, "I needed something to fill up the gap between those versions of her, something that would explain why her husband had left her or why her son hadn't been able to."[10] The last scene of *The Galton Case* has Teddy Federicks firmly telling her son, John Galton: "Don't bother about me."[11] She is "handing off"—relinquishing— her grown son to Sheila Howell, the young woman he can now love. It seems that Macdonald is expanding Freudian thinking about the family, arguing that it isn't only the child who has a series of tasks to progress through relating to how he loves his parents; parents too need to change the way they love their children, ever aware that those children become adolescents and then adults. If the intense love, for example, of a mother for her infant son doesn't change as the boy grows, then that mother is fixated, stymied in her own growth. And, of course, it's harder for a child to progress emotionally if his mother isn't keeping pace; it increases the peril of his being, like Stanley Broadhurst and Fritz Snow, sons who can't leave their mothers.

The explanations for Elizabeth and then Stanley's respective marital implosions go back still another generation. Archer learns that Elizabeth Falconer Broadhurst has written an overwrought memoir of her father, ending with the assessment: "Robert Driscoll Falconer, Jr., was a god come down to earth in human guise."[12] Another character tells Archer that Elizabeth "was a frozen woman, a daddy's girl."[13] There had been no sex in her marriage for ten years when Broadhurst left her.

Stanley has replicated that damaged dynamic of his family of origin. The novel's opening scene ends with Stanley leaving his wife and going off in a convertible in the company of a teenage girl, with his son as witness. Stanley's wife, Jean, tells Archer:

> My husband has been looking for his father for some time and gradually breaking up. Or maybe I've got it turned around. . . . He's angry at his father for abandoning him; at the same time he misses him and loves him. The two together can be paralyzing.[14]

A seconding opinion comes in a letter to Stanley from Reverend Lowell Riceyman:

> Your father chose to leave your mother and you, for reasons which neither you nor I can fathom. The heart has its reasons that the reason does not know.
>
> Think of your own life, Stanley. You have recently taken on the responsibilities of marriage. . . . Your wife is a fine and lovely girl, clearly more worthy of your living interest than those old passions of which you have written to me. The past can do very little for us—except in the end to release us. We must seek and accept release, and give release.[15]

But Stanley can't or won't: his obsessive search leads to his finding his father's grave, only to be murdered and buried there too, again with his son a witness. "A *déjà vu* feeling gave me a twinge of basic doubt, as if the burial and the digging-up might be repeated daily from now on,"[16] Archer remarks.

"I hoped it was over," Archer says on the last page of the novel. "I hoped Ronny's life wouldn't turn back toward his father's death as

his father's life had turned in a narrowing circle."[17] There is a courageous, if tentative, possibility for that in *The Underground Man*.

Macdonald's best novels close with the past acknowledged, the
present hopeful, and the future in sight. The books really are what
the journalist Jerry Tutunjian kidded Macdonald about: the same
story told twelve times. *The Galton Case* finishes with singing birds
and white rivers, a light in a window of a home, and John Galton and
his girlfriend setting off to golden California. Alex and Dolly Kincaid
are finally emotionally ready to begin their marriage in *The Chill*. The
final scene in *The Underground Man* is surprising: Archer is thinking
about becoming a husband and father himself. The last sentence is,
"Before night fell, Jean and I and Ronny drove out of town. . . . We
passed the steaming remnants of the fire and drove on south through
the rain."[18] According to Michael Kreyling, "Macdonald ends the
novel . . . with a powerfully ambivalent image":

> a cobbled-together basic family unit poised on the edge of
> assent. . . . Macdonald exits *The Underground Man* with
> Archer poised dangerously between the vulnerability of love
> and the certainty of ruin. . . . Archer himself begins to emerge,
> but warily, from his own personal underground, suspended be-
> tween isolation and connection.[19]

Earlier in the novel, when he first drives Jean to her mother-in-law's
ranch, Archer tells readers: "Her presence beside me sustained an
illusive feeling that there was an opening there into another time-
track or dimension. It had more future than the world I knew, and
not so bloody much traffic."[20]

It is worth noting that by the time Archer gets to *The Underground
Man*, he is a long way from the code-bound Op and Spade, and the
judgmental pilgrim Marlowe. Archer comes to believe that *The
Underground Man*'s Elizabeth, perfunctory wife and dependent
mother, murdered her husband by shooting him, but he decides not

to bear down on her for answers, much less turn her over to the police. It is indicative of an evolved Archer, one capable of moral charity:

> The hot breath of vengeance was growing cold in my nostrils as I grew older. I had more concern for a kind of economy in life that would help to preserve the things that were worth preserving.[21]

He is grateful for his decision when the medical examiner tells him that Leo didn't die of his gunshot wounds.

Macdonald believed that he, his wife, and then his daughter had suffered from parents still enmeshed in their own sad childhoods. Indeed, Linda said in reaction to a Rorschach image: "That made me think of a half-built life—and of my parents. I was mad when I thought they did not show me how to build my life. . . . I was mad at being forced to grow up—without help—I tried . . . but I didn't do well."[22] That repeated pattern—the son (Macdonald) "being forced to grow up—without help"—followed by the son's daughter (Linda) suffering the same experience was what Macdonald tried to save Jim Pagnusat from. It is hard to know what his grandson went through and why, but he dropped out of school at sixteen and died of a drug overdose at twenty-six in Las Vegas in 1989.

Fifty-three years and three generations before, Annie Moyer Millar had been naked in her son's college apartment. At her death, Macdonald had experienced several feelings: grandiose guilt, "black depression," "the necessity of not hurting anyone"—and an exhilarating "first grasp on manhood."[23] He was premature in claiming the last. Macdonald's childhood was still calling the shots. The greatest proofs of this were his decision to marry at twenty-three, just two years after Annie's death, and his choice of wife. Macdonald was still very much "the son," and Margaret Ellis Sturm was definitely "the son's wife."

He married a girl he knew in high school, a girl who had the childhood he resented:

My childhood was profoundly divided by the rich and the poor, the upright and the downcast, the sheep and the goats. We goats knew the moral pain influenced not so much by poverty as by the doctrine, still current, that poverty is always deserved.[24]

Margaret was student president of their class, the daughter of the mayor, winner of a classics scholarship, in the debate club, and on the school magazine's staff. In "Notes of a Son and Father," Macdonald is honest enough to admit, "He loved her for what she represented but also for herself."

Macdonald and Margaret went their separate ways after high school and then ran into each other five years later. Macdonald was an orphan now, bent on success and determined never to look back. Margaret may have been in that past he was rushing from, but she also had had a rough time of it since high school:

She was not in a good way. After several brilliant and arduous years at the University of "the City," a "nervous breakdown" had washed her out of the very difficult classics course. She had come to this other city to live with an aunt, had fallen out of a business course, had a mild schizophrenic episode, attempted suicide, was attempting to make new sense of her life by studying psychiatry and writing stories and verse.[25]

The nine words that follow the above description from "Notes of a Son and Father" are powerful: "The son knew his fate when he saw it." Macdonald's description of the buildup to their wedding is chilling; he must not have been able to see then what was so clear seventeen years later.

Within a few weeks they became lovers. She had had one previous lover, a doctor who seduced her and left her frigid. Her frigidity disappeared after some months. The son, with many backslidings—and she often hated him—considered their relationship a marriage, and began to try to be a husband. More than a year after its inception, and the day after he graduated from college, the marriage was legalized. Both knew that it meant this for the son-husband, that instead of going to Harvard or some such for graduate work, he would go to teachers' college and become a high school teacher. The choice was bitter but he embraced it (not without many later recriminations), fearing that if he "deserted" her for even as short a time as a year, she would perhaps kill herself or fall back into despair. [26]

It is all there. Macdonald didn't want Margaret when she was their high school's star; he wanted her after she had grown angry and prone to hysteria. Tom Nolan exclaims: "Only two years after his mother's death [Macdonald] was about to commit himself to an equally formidable and demanding relationship."[27] Macdonald's friend Bob Ford "'deplored' the idea of two such egotistical people marrying each other and predicted nothing but strain."[28]

Did this marriage happen under the auspices of Freud's Oedipus complex? Macdonald appears to have been sexually attracted to a woman like his mother. He also may have been operating in accord with the repetition compulsion, treating Margaret as he had treated his mother and finding a comforting familiarity in doing so. Part of Macdonald's anger at his father was at his having chosen a woman unfit for marriage and motherhood; maybe some of that anger at his father abated when he did the same thing.

"We re-create our childhood paradigm using three basic techniques," explains John D. Gartner:

We pick partners who are inclined to play their assigned roles; we provoke them to behave in these familiar old ways; and, finally, we project our past family figures onto them, distorting our perceptions to convince ourselves that they are behaving like figures from our childhood even when they are not. And, amazingly, we engineer all of this outside of our own awareness.[29]

And what about Margaret's attraction to Macdonald? What patterns from her childhood chimed again when she took him as her lover? Here is Macdonald again, from "Notes of a Son and Father":

Her father was a crude shrewd selfish self-made successful man who had gradually been humanized by misfortune, but not enough. In his early years he practiced a German authoritarianism in the home which fixed his daughter with, among other problems, a permanent eating problem, and a long hatred for him only lately tempered by tolerance. The mother, whom the father truly loved, was a woman of great goodness but poor insight. She passed her last seven years or so dying slowly and horribly of cancer, and masterminding, with a rod of silk, her brilliant daughter's life. Everything the daughter did, and she was immensely active in music ("concert pianist"), school politics, her studies (she learned six years of Greek in her final year of high school, and went to college on a scholarship, the family having just lost its money partly through the depredations of her older brother who was a psychopathic personality, forger, alcoholic, and who died under a freight train five years ago: there was some incestuous content, not likely overt, in the love of brother and sister)— everything the daughter did, she did for her mother, almost literally as if the mother's life depended on it.

Macdonald and Margaret thought with the excited logic of smart students and the erotic illogic of new lovers that they would be each other's salvation. Macdonald wrote her that they shared Kierkegaard's worldview. For her part, Margaret said that he felt like "my other, better half, my miraculous twin."[30] They were counting on each other. But they had suffered hard beginnings and were therefore more likely to play their histories out again as adults. Gartner explains: "The theory has it that recreating the traumatic situation allows us to feel a sense of mastery over it. It's not being done to us. We're doing it, which allows us to feel more in control."[31]

Within three months of the wedding, she was pregnant. "That's when you really feel the entrapment," Margaret said later, "You know: 'Here I am—*stuck*.' "[32] For his part, Macdonald was afraid of passing on his mother's hysteria.[33]

Linda was born in 1939, and they thought she was beautiful. Her exhausted new parents were self-aware enough to know that they lacked models of good parenting and believed that they couldn't trust their own inclinations. They argued about how to raise Linda: Margaret followed behaviorist John Broadus Watson's strictures of letting babies cry and making do with less kissing and holding; Macdonald "thought these notions were nuts."[34] They were exceedingly self-conscious parents, yet they unconsciously and compulsively repeated patterns from their largely disastrous families of origin. Macdonald admits to his psychoanalyst: "Mother and father have never shared a room, because father snores and wife is nervous."[35] But, like Macdonald and his mother sharing a bed, Margaret and Linda shared a bedroom until the latter was eleven years old. (Margaret and Macdonald never shared one.) Meanwhile, like her mother before her, Margaret, according to a family friend,

> was always revving Linda's engine as it were, stepping on the accelerator of her personality, making her *do* all sorts of things,

making her a bit of a show-off. . . . with Linda the box was always open, as it were, with people looking in, expecting, commenting, constantly stimulating in ways that somehow or other made for a nervous youngster.[36]

Macdonald admits, "Present resentment and the ill past sometimes made him cruel to the child. He would shake her sometimes; sometimes he slapped her face, in lieu of his wife's."[37] And it all somehow had to do with sex, Macdonald began to realize, when his daughter was sixteen.

It was a doubled, self-defeating dynamic that was operating in Macdonald's early work and marriage. On the conscious level, he was fascinated by and well versed in psychological scholarship. In 1947 Macdonald tried to write a "serious" autobiographical novel about "an adolescent boy [William] being shoved into delinquency by social and economic pressure."[38] *Winter Solstice* doesn't work because social and economic pressures are influences from the outside and less potent than those within William, and because when the author tried to draw upon his own past to address William's unhappy behavior, he only got angry. Macdonald never sent *Winter Solstice* to a publisher, calling it "a mass of undigested pain."[39]

The Three Roads (1948)—one of Macdonald's early, pre-Archer novels—takes its title from the three roads that intersected in Phocis, where Oedipus killed his father. *The Three Roads* comes from Macdonald's reading and is heavily influenced by Graham Greene's sometimes surreal novel, *The Ministry of Fear* (1943), wherein Arthur Rowe is haunted by having murdered his wife years before and believes that someone is trying to kill him, even as London is being bombed on all sides. What *The Three Roads* is not drawn from is Macdonald's own life experience.

Macdonald's 1952 dissertation is titled "The Inward Eye: A Revaluation of Coleridge's Psychological Criticism." (Before settling on this topic, he tried to finish Coleridge's famously unfinished poem, "Christobel." Macdonald was thereafter grateful that his attempt had been lost to time.) He focuses on the shift from the Age of Faith, as defined by Augustine, Aquinas, and Dante, to the Enlightenment of Descartes, Marx, and Darwin. These latter three effectively ended "the hand of God" as the link between the seen and the unseen. Macdonald argues that Coleridge was "groping toward the universal model of the unconscious by way of human beings' response to stimulation of the imagination." Coleridge therefore was "Freud's indispensable precursor."[40] And Macdonald, some four years before his crisis and psychoanalysis, was already versed in and championing Freud. But, as is the case in *The Three Roads*, Macdonald himself can't be located in his dissertation. Late in his life, Macdonald would say that he thought his last novels were better on Freud than was "The Inward Eye."

Macdonald and Margaret wrote a never-optioned screenplay together—a family romance, really—called "The Mastermind." It is about a former ethics professor who is now president of a Midwestern college, his irreverent wife, and their brainy daughter—in short, who the Macdonalds wanted to be. However, the compulsion to repeat childhood paradigms acted as an overriding and hidden agenda, insidiously undercutting their best efforts to do differently, to be better as husband and wife, father and mother than their parents had been before them.

What happened to Margaret in her young marriage made her angry for years, and understandably so. In 1940—in cold Kitchener, Ontario—where Macdonald taught high school English and history, Margaret faltered, beset by ailments that she later admitted were probably psychosomatic. She went to bed, and her husband brought home dozens of mystery novels from the public library. Margaret thought, "I could do this." She and Macdonald brainstormed some plots and settings; she concocted a handsome, William Blake-quoting psychiatrist/detective; and then she started to work. The new mother—who had prepared for submission to American magazines thirty-five of her husband's short sketches, verse, and stories for youths to American magazines during Linda's first six weeks at home—now wrote a sixty-thousand-word detective novel in fifteen days, followed by two or three complete rewrites. She later said, "I had to do something to get out of that bed. To get out of that *town*."[41] *The Invisible Worm*, sold to Doubleday for $250, followed by *The Weak-Eyed Bat* and *The Devil Loves Me* in 1942, was indeed their ticket out—that and the teaching fellowship and doctoral program the University of Michigan offered Macdonald. Like his fellow California-born John Galton, Macdonald went back over the border in 1941.

Macdonald landed in Visiting Professor W. H. Auden's course, Fate and the Individual in European History. Auden, who was influenced by Freud and Carl Jung and who would write the celebrated essay "The Guilty Vicarage: Notes on the Detective Story" in 1948, became a mentor. Auden's respect for the detective story lent gravitas to "Margaret's genre" in Macdonald's mind. According to Tom Nolan, though, Macdonald was uneasy about Auden's homosexuality and turned down his offer to introduce Macdonald around Manhattan. The homosexuality was there in Macdonald's childhood and coming of age; it was an urge he had left behind, absolutely and without comment.

In 1944 Macdonald, echoing his father, went to war in the Pacific. While gone from home, he sent Margaret his reaction to reading Karen Horney, "I don't regard myself as a neurotic (nor you either). . . . Concerning my basic motivations I'm pretty well fouled up. I think I know what will satisfy me . . . but I don't know *why*."[42] Margaret replied with love letters:

> Oh Lord, it seems like a dream; but it *isn't*—after the war we'll *both* write; we'll share the housework and write ourselves silly. There are certain things I'd like to do before we start to write, but they'll be easy, natural, biological and *wonderful*. . . .We just *fit*, that's all.[43]

She signed one letter "Chuckles" and another "Your big blonde."[44]

Margaret kept writing: it got them out of Ann Arbor and "the whole academic thing,"[45] which she disliked. While Macdonald was off in the Navy, she made enough money to buy them a house she picked out in a California town she had found, Santa Barbara. Margaret was the breadwinner and the success in the family. That changed; Macdonald came home and stole her accomplishment. He wrote better detective novels than she did.

Margaret eventually published twenty-eight books; she became a well-reviewed, financially successful, sophisticated writer. Her work is quick, glib, fun, and mean. Most of her detectives are amateurs who don't narrate, unlike the hired and hard-boiled Op, Marlowe, and Archer. What fascinated Margaret were psychopathic personalities and their victims—not the idealized investigator. In *The Fiend*, the eponymous man at its center likes children: "The conditions were impossible, of course. He couldn't turn and run in the opposite direction every time he saw a child. They were all over, everywhere, at any hour."[46] And then a child disappears.

Her early books are lighter and funnier, followed by some more seriously gothic and psychological and, finally, by works that are an amalgam of satire and psychosis. None of them has heroines or heroes, and Margaret's dead-on, confident, biting voice is present every time. In her best-known novel, *Beast in View*, a character gets called a liar and replies, "Oh, that. Sure."[47]

And that is a piece of what Margaret was: a strong personality who never hesitated to say what she knew. Donald Pearce opined that "she needed praise; didn't want competition. For all her strength of mind and rhinocerine will, she had a fragile ego. Someone who was compulsively difficult."[48]

Eudora Welty was a sunnier soul, a quieter, less competitive writer, and she wasn't married to Ross Macdonald. In January 1971, he wrote to thank Welty, whom he didn't know, for her *New York Times* review of *The Underground Man*: "As you know a writer and his work don't really exist until they've been read. You have given me the fullest and most explicit reading I've ever had, or that I ever expected. I exist as a writer more completely thanks to you."[49] In May of that same year, Macdonald and Welty met by chance in the lobby of the Algonquin Hotel, and they spent a magical night: at a cocktail party hosted by Alfred Knopf and then talking and walking, up and down Broadway. The night expanded into the happiest, easiest, and healthiest romantic relationship Macdonald ever had. As for Welty, Macdonald was the love of her life. Her friend, writer Reynolds Price, tells what he was privy to:

> One night he and I had a few drinks and were sitting in the motel in Jackson when this one particular very memorable moment occurred. We were talking about Eudora and what a wonderful person she was; and I went on you know about how important she'd been to me. . . . And [Macdonald] stopped me and said, "No, you don't understand. I'm saying I love her as a woman." And I'll take a Bible oath that he said that to me. . . . I think that for both of them this was an emotional relationship of *great* importance, in both their lives. She took great delight in him, too. . . . I think she was a great romance of [Macdonald's] life, at the end of his life. And [Macdonald] was of great importance to Eudora Welty; I think it ran very deep for her. My own sense is that they were in love with one another. And it was late in both their lives.[50]

The affair lasted twelve years—until Macdonald died. It consisted of visits in Santa Barbara and Jackson, books dedicated to each other, and love letters. After he was gone, biographer Ralph Sipper urged Welty to publish both sides of their correspondence: "Someday the confluence (it *is* a wonderful word) of your lives should, in my view, be a matter of human record. What you and [Macdonald] exchanged was a pureness that need not be buried."[51] Sipper was wooing Welty with her own word, "confluence," from *The Optimist's*

Daughter and *One Writer's Beginnings*. But he had no luck; she quietly refused. (Later, the two writers' estates changed course, and publication of their correspondence took place in July 2015.)

The affair brought perhaps only a qualified happiness. Or maybe it is that the pleasures in a long affair or friendship are different from the joy of a marriage that prevails. Perhaps all happiness is qualified. Macdonald has Archer say in *The Doomsters*: "I'd like to see that house destroyed, and that family scattered forever."[52] In *The Blue Hammer*, he wrote, "There are certain families whose members should all live in different towns—different states, if possible—and write each other letters once a year."[53] Yet Welty and Macdonald probably never consummated their affair, and Macdonald never left Margaret. "I guess I don't believe in endings," he wrote to a friend going through a bad time in his own marriage.[54]

H ammett did not believe in marriage and ended his own. He said monogamy was unnatural and untenable for men. Hammett's plots have a curious trajectory, wherein violence and sex both ramp up as the detective/hero loses control. Over and over in Hammett's fiction, there turns out to be mortal danger in a man's letting down his guard, particularly in the presence of his wife. These women don't enjoy sex. They have it for other, dangerous-to-men reasons. The sole exception is Nora Charles, who is a member of the most demoralizing hard-boiled sorority of all: wives with money.

Women who aren't wives are treacherous too but often they are more straightforward about it all. "I gathered she was strictly pay-as-you-enter,"[55] the Op says about the prostitute Dinah Brand in *Red Harvest*. Dinah charges by the hour for sex or information, and then invests her income in successful stocks. She's seedy and greedy but unapologetically corrupt and utterly transparent; Hammett, who hated sanctimony and artifice, no doubt loved her. But in *The Dain Curse*, the other Op novel, the married Alice Dain is a sexual savage:

> This was a blonde whose body was rounded . . . with the cushioned, soft-sheathed muscles of the hunting cats, whether in jungle or alley. . . . She was simple as an animal, with an animal's simple ignorance of right and wrong, dislike for being thwarted, and spitefulness when trapped.[56]

The Dain Curse is a strange, three-part tale with a forgettable—because pure female—perpetual victim. In Part One, the Op figures out that once upon a time, four-year-old Gabrielle Leggett got tricked into killing her own mother. In Part Two, the Op rescues the now-grown, morphine-addicted Gabrielle from the California-slick "Temple of the Holy Grail." In Part Three, Gabrielle is a newlywed until her husband gets murdered. This time the Op gets it right for good: a novelist murdered Gabrielle's groom and her aunt/stepmother; he also got her addicted to morphine and took her to the temple. Gabrielle just gets flung from part to part. Sinda Gregory agrees: "She is passive and helpless to the point of catatonia, unable to control or interpret anything that happens around her, and constantly needing men to rescue her from other men."[57]

Hammett has figured out how to write a fun, good woman by the time Effie Perine shows up in *The Maltese Falcon*. But Sam Spade is tempted by and beds canny Brigid O'Shaughnessy. Nevertheless, he later turns her in for murdering his partner: she saw the sex as a quid pro quo; he did not. For both Alice Dain in *The Dain Curse* and O'Shaughnessy in *The Maltese Falcon*, sex is the weapon they use to get something else.

Hammett's view of sex and love is even more jaded in *The Glass Key*. Ned Beaumont leaves town with the girl at the end but, as Peter Wolfe describes it in his study of Hammett:

The book's last two sentences read, "Janet Henry looked at Ned Beaumont. He stared fixedly at the door. . . ." His inexpressiveness is well judged. Sex can kill you dead. To show a woman love is to ask for trouble. . . . The first time they met, . . . she began panther-tracking him.[58]

Sex and violence are urges from the same primal ("panther-tracking") source—it is women doing the tracking and the murdering, and money is in the mix.

Violence is innocent in Hammett's first de facto novel: *Black Mask* published two long stories, "The Big Knock-Over," and its sequel, "$106,000 Blood Money," in February and May 1927. The stories are full of exuberant mayhem: the most successful 100 criminals "from all over Rand-McNally"[59] meet in San Francisco and simultaneously stick up two major banks across the street from each other. Here's who dies: sixteen cops, twelve bystanders and bank clerks, and seven robbers. Forty-eight cops are hurt, and thirty-one dinged-up crooks are put in jail. It's a funny premise, and the wily brains behind the knock-over, a little old Greek named Papadopoulos, tricks the Op into letting him go at the end. The stories are a hoot; the violence is light-hearted; and there aren't any women.

The body count begins to go down—*Red Harvest* has twenty-four murders, *The Dain Curse* twelve—but the violence turns sick, and the Op gets compromised. Ned Beaumont is beaten for days, nearly to death in *The Glass Key*; finally left alone, he breaks down and attempts suicide. One of the hard-boiled protocols has been breached, leaving the reader disoriented and queasy.

The Thin Man, the one that spawned so many spin-offs, is an unsatisfactory last novel whose meaning is found just under the double entendres and cocktails. Nick Charles doesn't work and lives on his wife's money. If he weren't cynical, he wouldn't be hard-boiled at all.

"The hard-boiled detective sets out to investigate a crime," writes John G. Cawelti in *Adventure, Mystery and Romance: Formula Stories as Art and Popular Culture*, "but invariably finds that he must go beyond the solution to some kind of personal choice of action."[60] The personal choices—and the fictional detectives' vaunted personal codes—have to do with violence, anger, and sex.

Hammett was uneasy about all three. He feared that he had a tendency to hurt people: hence his rules against fighting, shooting, and driving. He certainly knew he was an angry drunk. He shied away from monogamy and appears to have been more comfortable as an exuberant womanizer. Hammett was productive and happy in exclusively male enclaves.

Hammett's only wife is downplayed in the biographies, much less in the critical studies. Jose was a hard-luck kid—the first child of an alcoholic coal miner and his wife—who grew up in Basin, Montana. Six months after the couple's third baby was born, Jose's mother died. Relatives in Butte took in the infant, and he died there before his first birthday. How did a four-year-old process that second loss? Maybe Jose thought that her mother went missing and then the baby disappeared into the horizon, looking for her. Jose was six and Walter four when their father, Hubert, died. The children were already farmed out to neighbors, and Jose was mothering Walter. It is understandable that she didn't expect her father's death would change her life. I will take care of Walter and nobody has to take care of me, she may have thought. But nuns came and took the children to an orphanage in Helena, where Jose kept Walter right with her. Now he and she were members of a sad category: surrendered children. Eighty years later Hammett biographer William F. Nolan would use an oxymoron, "an unworldly orphan,"[61] to describe Jose.

In 1905 Hubert's sister and brother-in-law grudgingly took Jose, now seven, and Walter into their home in Anaconda. The Kellys already had twelve children and, on her first night in that big house, Jose took into her bed the toddler who had been supplanted by a newborn.[62] The next day she started in on the housework. Jose knew two things: seismic shifts came without warning and were always bad. Besides, she already had her code: work hard and be a mother to somebody. She got through eighth grade and talked her way into a nursing school that required their students to have two years of high school and be eighteen. As her daughter Jo wrote about Jose, "Her options were limited. Staying with the Kellys was not one of them."[63]

It should be lost on nobody that Jose fell in love with Hammett when he was under her care in the Cushman Institute—a Public Health Service hospital in Tacoma, Washington—and that Hammett's beloved mother was also a nurse. He followed Jose around; he was her private orderly. He took her on walks and ferry rides. Mostly they just talked. Later she remembered, "Of all the patients, [he] seemed to stand out. I thought he was very intelligent and striking. . . . Also he was very gentle."[64] After Hammett was transferred to a veteran's hospital in California, they wrote to each other. Letters that had been published made it clear that Hammett and Jose lived on that correspondence. Somewhere in those Cushman months, Jose got pregnant—not so very surprising. Hospitals, especially sanitariums for long-term patients, are worlds unto themselves. In novelist Andrea Barrett's *The Air We Breathe*, set in a 1916 sanitarium, she wrote:

> We lived as if we were already dead, as if we'd died when we were diagnosed and nothing we did after that mattered. We lived as if nothing was important.[65]

In Sue Miller's novel *The World Below*, set in a sanitarium in 1919, she wrote of sex "in hunger and terror and a kind of willed abandon."[66] Hammett was already an exuberant womanizer; he had been treated for gonorrhea as a teenager. He was, however, an equal opportunity philanderer; he never held promiscuity against the women he loved.

What matters is that they loved each other: he and Jose were friends, and she was pregnant. She wrote to Hammett, who wrote back, "Come to San Francisco and I will marry you." And she did and he did. On their wedding day, she wrote that "he bought me flowers"[67]—and Mary was born in October, all in 1921.

The pregnancy only became an issue seventy-one years later when Mary died, and Jose and Hammett were already gone. Lillian Hellman abruptly claimed that Mary was not Hammett's child, that Jose had had an affair with a different soldier and that when she came up pregnant, she wrote to Hammett. He had played knight-errant and married Jose, Hellman contended. Trying to debunk Hellman's assertion, the Hammett family proffered an incomplete Hammett-to-Jose letter written in May 1921:

> I didn't know if you were a "wild woman" or not before I went out with you, Lady, but I did know that you were a wonderful little person from head to heels, from shoulder to shoulder, from back-bone to wishbone, inside and . . . [68]

However, excerpts from a March 1921 Hammett-to-Jose letter might have alluded to Jose's having denied him sex:

> [W]e ought to be out on the bridge . . . staging our customary friendly, but now and then a bit rough, dispute over the relative merits of "yes" and "no. . . . " if I'm ever to get it [a picture Jose had promised to send] I'll most likely have to come up and take it away from you. Maybe that's what I should have done about something else I wanted.[69]

It is hard to know. Hammett was a rare man who could have made such a decision quietly and then abided by it for the rest of his life. Any reader of Hammett's fiction can imagine that the inventor of the Op and Sam Spade could have seen the chance to do a good thing for a good woman and a child and simply done it. On the other hand, this is the kind of lie that Hellman was likely to tell, and she long wanted to deny that Hammett ever had loved Jose or had considered her and their children his family.

Hammett's granddaughter, Julie Marshall Rivett, says that Hellman's "disclosure" was sad.[70] True or not, neither Hammett nor Jose ever would have wanted it said. Hellman would have known this when she decided to say what she did.

The San Francisco years, the writing years, and the marriage years were one and the same, 1921 to 1929. The realities of a domestic situation with children mandated a work ethic, a responsibility-laden and scheduled-every-day lifestyle that made possible—and, in a sense, necessary—the writing of sixty stories and four novels in eight years. Hammett wanted badly to do what his father hadn't; he wanted to support his family reliably.

The Hammetts began living apart in 1928 on the order of his doctors, who believed Hammett's frequently active and thereby contagious tuberculosis endangered his family. Soon enough his disease went into remission, and the reason for the separation became an excuse for an arrangement that suited Hammett better—and that was the tipping point in their marriage. For the next two years, they all lived in San Francisco, but not together. Jose had a husband who came and went. Hammett was still writing to Jose thirty-three years later, in the year he died.

In 1929 Hammett hatched a plan: he put Jose and the girls on the train to Los Angeles where, so this new excuse had it, she would like the weather. Besides, he would frequently be in Hollywood, writing for the movies. You take care of the girls and I'll take care of you,

Hammett told Jose. Then he hopped the train to New York with a pulp novelist named Nell Martin. In 1930 *The Maltese Falcon* was dedicated "To Jose," but Hammett rarely lived with her again. Jose, people said, was the woman Hammett outgrew.

When Hammett met Jose in a hospital in Washington, he was an unpromising prospect: active tuberculosis, an eighth-grade education, no money, and a peripatetic resume. Ten years later when Hammett met Hellman in Hollywood, he was the man of the hour in the sexiest city in the world: an accomplished writer, a strikingly handsome older man, and happily spending all his money.

As for Hellman, she was young, smart, determined to write, and willing to live recklessly when she met Hammett. She was also preternaturally angry; in *Pentimento* she recalls a childhood friend asking, "Are you as angry a woman as you were a child?"[71] When Hammett pushed, she pushed back; he liked that. For her part, she fell prey to her own variety of repetition compulsion:

> Fearing infidelity, as her father had been unfaithful to her
> mother, Lily had chosen the quintessentially unfaithful man.
> It was an attempt to re-create the primal experience hoping
> it would turn out differently. Of course, it could not.[72]

Hammett's kneejerk, rigid response to those three minor instances of violence was echoed, tellingly, in another realm in 1942: one night Hammett was drunk and pawing at Hellman. She told him "she wouldn't sleep with him when he was like this." Hammett's response was a unilateral decision never to make love to her again.[73]

In the thirty years they had together, they lived apart for extended months and sometimes years, had sex with other people, drank too much, and she raged at him and he went elsewhere. They were active communists together, he taught her how to write, and she cared for him when he was dying. It was an enduring, remarkable love affair.

Cissy Pascal was a wife of a different stripe to Raymond Chandler, whom she married less than two weeks after his mother's death in 1923. Chandler listed his age on the marriage register as thirty-six, which he was; Cissy listed herself as forty-three, which she was not. She was fifty-four, and he didn't know. What people eventually said was that Chandler "married his mother," but he did not see that. Like Macdonald, who married an emotionally ill-equipped woman, and Hammett, who married a motherly nurse, Chandler may have wanted an older woman to "get it right" this time—"it" being the fact that he was under his mother's thumb. In Freudian parlance, Chandler may have fallen sway to the repetition compulsion, which further involved treating Cissy as he had treated his mother—all this despite his wife's being unlike Florence Chandler.

Pearl Eugenia Hurlburt was born in tiny Perry Township, Ohio: 12,000 people, dairy cows, and a cheese factory were there. Many Hurlburts still live there but—as soon as she could—Pearl got out. She moved to Harlem and thrived. She changed her name to Cissy and made money playing the piano and modeling nude for art classes. She would stay single longer than most women at the time and marry and divorce twice, both at her instigation. She wed a salesman named Leon Porcher, called a halt to the relationship after seven years, and Leon didn't appear in court on the day of the divorce.

Seven years later, in 1912, Cissy married again, and this marriage meant more. Julian Pascal (who had changed his name too, from Goodridge Bowen) was an eminent concert pianist and composer, a former professor at the Guildhall School of Music in London. A vaguely defined emotional condition called "neurasthenia"—marked by lassitude, fatigue, headaches, and irritability—had ended his London acclaim. Hoping a change would help, Pascal relocated to

Manhattan, where he met Cissy. Within a year of their marriage, Pascal tried yet another change, this one in climate. He and Cissy moved to Los Angeles, where Cissy met Raymond Chandler. Chandler was not, in all, a handsome man, but there was a golden pocket of years when he was, and one of those was 1913. He was twenty-five, healthy, tan—vital. Julian was aging quickly, his years of renown in the past. By 1913 he was a tired, crabby, and nervous music teacher.

Cissy and Chandler's new marriage was happy. They went ballroom dancing, took drives in Chandler's fancy car, had pet names for each other, and collected little glass animals. Chandler, who was uneasy and obsessive about intimacy in any form, could relax with his comfortably sexy wife. She did her housework naked, was perfumed, and wore theatrically feminine clothes: "Cissy kept a stagily erotic pink boudoir, filled with Hollywood-style French furniture and a pink ruffled bedspread."[74]

Warren Lloyd came through again and got Chandler a bookkeeping job with Dabney Oil. Chandler decided to be a successful businessman, and for ten years he was. Somewhere in those years, though, he began to drink in an implacable way. There were blackouts, manic episodes, and middle-of-the-night phone calls to friends threatening suicide. Yet the ramped-up drinking helped his sexual excitability, and Chandler bedded younger office girls. "You know how it is with marriage—any marriage," says a character in *The Lady in the Lake*. "After a while a guy like me, a common no-good guy like me, he wants to feel a leg. Some other leg. Maybe it's lousy, but that's the way it is."[75] At work, Chandler was warned, and then warned again. In the depths of the Depression, Chandler was fired for chronic alcoholism and absenteeism. Biographer Frank MacShane notes:

> Chandler never denied his dismissal, but he did not give the real reason for it. "My service cost them too much," he once said. "Always a good reason for letting a man go."

[E]xactly twenty years after his return to America he was back where he began, except that he had a bad reputation, fewer possibilities, and less energy than before.[76]

He moved out on February 3, 1930, and took off back to Seattle where he had a Canadian army friend. He stopped drinking. Cissy was not about to be a victim, and by March 8, 1930, she had a Memorandum of Agreement—a property settlement between herself and Chandler—notarized.

Two years later Cissy was hospitalized with pneumonia, and Chandler came back right away. That was their marriage's first tipping point: not that he came back but that he came because she was sick and thereby needed rescue. They rented an apartment on Greenwood Place; it was the fifteenth place Chandler had lived since coming to Los Angeles, and he would live in twenty-one other places in Los Angeles and La Jolla before his death. Maybe dislocation felt right to a man who was born in America to Irish parents and then raised in England.

The hard-boiled stories Chandler had started to write while legally separated from his wife contain a number of threatening women. Here is the beginning paragraph of "Red Wind":

There was a desert wind blowing that night. It was one of those hot dry Santa Anas that come down through the mountain passes and curl your hair and make your nerves jump and your skin itch. On nights like that every booze party ends in a fight. Meek little wives feel the edge of the carving knife and study their husbands' necks. Anything can happen.[77]

The short stories came first and were Chandler's training ground. The strengths of those stories are sympathetic character study, meticulous and apt description, the language of emotion, dialogue in the vernacular, imposition of literary sensibility, and sense of place twinned to loneliness. As good as his short stories are, the novels are better. All of the stories' strengths grow stronger still in his novels. The novels have that friendless raconteur and doomed romantic hero Philip Marlowe, and he makes all the difference. "As soon as he was free of the short-story restrictions imposed by the cheaper pulps," says Clive James in his Chandler essay, "The Country Behind the Hill," "his way of writing quickly found its outer limits: all he needed to do was refine it. The main refining instrument was Marlowe's personality."[78]

It is Marlowe's behaviors around women and gay men that largely define him. The women he rescues are in troubles of their own making. In Chandler's first novel, *The Big Sleep*, Vivian Sternwood has a missing bootlegger husband and gambling debts. Her sister Carmen is a sexy psychopath with

> little sharp predatory teeth. . . . Her eyes were wide open. The dark slate color of the iris had devoured the pupil. They were mad eyes. . . . The tinny chuckling noise was still coming from her and a little froth oozed down her chin. . . . The hissing sound grew louder and her face had that scraped bone look. Aged, deteriorated, became animal, and not a nice animal.[79]

When Marlowe finds her nude and giggling in his apartment, he "tore the bed to pieces savagely."[80] Crime novelist and Chandler's English solicitor, Michael Gilbert, says that "Carmen is the first in a long line of little witches that runs right through the novels, just as her big sister, Vivian, is the first in a long line of rich bitches who find that Marlowe is the only thing money can't buy."[81]

In *Farewell, My Lovely*, Velma Grayle is the murderer: a "blonde to make a bishop kick a hole in a stained-glass window."[82] She is Marlowe's type: "I like smooth shiny girls, hard-boiled and loaded with sin,"[83] he says. She is also an animal: "When I got to her mouth it was half open and burning and her tongue was a darting snake between her teeth."[84] *The Lady in the Lake* has the requisite Chandler murderess, but he saves the more memorable description for the lady in the lake:

> The thing rolled over once more and an arm flapped up barely above the skin of the water and the arm ended in a bloated hand that was the hand of a freak. Then the face came. A swollen pulpy gray white mass without features, without eyes, without mouth. A blotch of gray dough, a nightmare with human hair on it.[85]

Chandler's fictional women are often evil in ways verging on the fantastical.

Chandler fancied himself and Marlowe as lovers, by which he means men who protect and honor women. Reverence, however, is a distancing, self-protecting, doubled stance. Hammett's detectives know they have uncomfortable capacities for violence against men and are wary of sex because they know women use it to control men. But Chandler's canon includes troubling combinations of violence and sex. As Wolfe argues,

> A darker manifestation of Chandler's sexual fears is the recurrence in his work of violence directed to women. . . . Even in hardboiled fiction, such violence is rare. It can't be explained by saying that the detective's contempt for civil law had driven him to seek redress privately. Lew Archer never hit a woman, nor did Sam Spade.[86]

In *The Long Goodbye*, Eileen Wade beats Sylvia Lennox's face to a "bloody sponge"[87] and then comes after Marlowe:

> "Put me on the bed," she breathed.
> I did that. Putting my arms around her I touched bare skin, soft skin, soft, yielding flesh. I lifted her and carried her the

few steps to the bed and lowered her. She kept her arms around my neck. She was making some kind of whistling noise in her throat. Then she thrashed about and moaned. This was murder. I was erotic as a stallion.[88]

Chandler's women are often bestial murderers and only Marlowe is man enough to take them down violently or sexually—except that he doesn't because he keeps women away, on pedestals. If the women he writes about are evil enough, then Marlowe's detachment is rational and not odd. Somehow, Chandler is insisting, these clashing axioms are all true.

In 1932 Cissy not only took her estranged husband back; she agreed to his chancy plan to write fiction for a living. Although Chandler had drunk his way out of the second business job Lloyd had found for him, now Lloyd gave Chandler $100 a month until he was self-sufficient. In his unmoored Seattle years, Chandler had discovered the pulps. The man with the accountant's mindset now decided to be a pulp writer; it took him five months to write his first short story, "Blackmailers Don't Shoot," which he rewrote five times. Joseph T. Shaw was nothing but happy: "All I did was buy it; Chandler had done all the work and the skill and talent existed on paper from his first page!"[89]

Chandler would write eighteen more short stories before concocting Philip Marlowe for *The Big Sleep* in 1938. By then his marriage had become an overlay of his childhood experience with his mother, in ways he could not have foreseen when he and Cissy got married in 1924. As a little boy, he had believed that he had rescued Florence from a terrible marriage and must care for her ever after because she was somehow unable to care for herself. He had done that. When his mother died after a long illness, he quickly married the sexy, red-haired, independent woman he loved. In 1938, he knew that his wife was not seven years his senior but seventeen years—she was truly old enough to have been his mother—and Cissy was sick with a chronic, degenerative lung disease.

In 1930 she was ready to divorce him but in 1932 she took Chandler back: maybe because she was sick, maybe because he wasn't drinking, and maybe because the first four years of their marriage had been happy ones. As of 1938, Chandler had published seventeen well-received stories, and he had been sober and faithful. And so Cissy would continue to devote herself wholly to him, encouraging Chandler's romantic notion that he was her rescuing hero, calling him "Raymio" and "Gallibeoth." Freeman argues that

Cissy nurtured the sense he had of himself as her white knight whose task it was to stand as the moral force in the corrupted universe, of which Los Angeles . . . was perfectly emblematic. He would not have become the writer he did had he not had this vision of himself to impart to his fictional hero, and he needed Cissy to fulfill this idea, just as he needed Los Angeles to provide him with atmosphere and stories.[90]

It is important to see that Chandler already had a romantic sense of himself before Cissy and Marlowe. Chandler was hell-bent on being a rescuer because this is what he knew from his early childhood; thus, he could not help but believe that he had rescued his wife. And when Chandler invented his fictional better self, Marlowe, of course he made him a paladin.

Eventually, however, there was weariness in Chandler's devotion. In the 1939 story "I'll Be Waiting," Miss Cressy, the redheaded, has-been singer responds when asked if she contemplated suicide, "Redheads don't jump, Tony. They hang on—and wither."[91] By 1942 Cissy was seventy-two; Chandler, fifty-four, wrote a poem, "Kashinmor the Elephant," named for two of the "amuels," which is what the Chandlers called the many tiny glass animals they collected.

His lady is not young
Her smile is thin and tarnished filigree
Mascara melts beneath her haggard eyes
Between her breasts the powder dampened lines.
He will lie still and hear her snore again
Filling the night with particles of pain
He will lie still and listen to her flute,
With the face of a stillborn child that no one loved.[92]

In 1954's *The Long Goodbye*, Eileen Wade's suicide note includes the following sentences: "Time makes everything mean and shabby and wrinkled. The tragedy of life . . . is not that the beautiful things die young, but that they grow old and mean."[93]

Certainly there could be an edge to Cissy's constancy too: she "had not particularly liked" *The Big Sleep*,[94] his first novel, published in 1939, nor in fact any of those that followed. Also in 1939, Chandler set down a detailed plan for future work: he would write three more detective novels, a dramatic novel, and a set of six or seven "short-long stories." He showed his list to Cissy, who added a note: "Dear Raymio, you'll have fun looking at this maybe, and seeing what useless dreams you had. Or perhaps it will not be fun."[95]

So, in 1943 Chandler went to Hollywood to co-write *Double Indemnity*. Soon he was losing ground again to alcoholism and womanizing. It all smelled like the oil business days, but this time the Chandlers didn't separate. This was their marriage's second and last tipping point because this time Cissy stayed in it. David Wyatt writes in "Chandler, Marriage, and the Great Wrong Place":

It is nearly impossible to imagine the life Cissy managed to live during these years, shuttled about as she was from flat to flat, without friends, or money, or work of her own. She has no voice that has survived. She collected editions of her husband's work. Above all, she stayed.[96]

It was a shocking, sustained capitulation for a woman who had been such an extrovert, such a vibrant presence. Chandler's fiction and his marriage hold profound doublenesses. Cissy had tricked her husband into marrying her by not telling him she was seventeen years older than he was. Somewhere in the long years of their marriage, Chandler learned of this lie and began to deal with it, although in complex ways.

How did Macdonald, Hammett, and Chandler experience love and where are the parallels in their fiction? The three writers did almost all—and clearly the best—of their writing while living with their wives. Each man unwittingly wed under the influence of a repetition compulsion, marrying women with whom they could re-enact their first childhood encounters with love. Margaret Millar brought her own repetition compulsion and fragile emotional health to her angry marriage. She influenced Macdonald's decisions to write detective stories—she went first—and undergo psychoanalysis—an endeavor that she believed in. Jose Hammett, with her quiet work ethic and even temperament, tacitly discouraged her husband's self-destructive tendencies, and she and her elder daughter may have been the recipients of a great, unspoken act of generosity on Hammett's part. Cissy Chandler devoted herself wholly to her husband and nurtured his need to believe that he was a romantic figure who rescued women.

Hammett, Chandler, and Macdonald stayed uneasily married. Hammett and Macdonald found estimable lovers, Lillian Hellman and Eudora Welty. Chandler was an inveterate womanizer but didn't look for his own true lover. The question is obvious: why didn't he?

Jose Dolan, c. 1915. She talked her way into a nursing program for which students had to be 18 (she was 15) and have two years of high school (she had none). (Courtesy of Josephine Hammett Marshall)

Dashiell and Jose Hammett's daughters, Mary and Jo, c. 1930. His daughters drove some of the best of Hammett's biography. (Courtesy of Josephine Hammett Marshall)

Dashiell Hammett, 1933. The man Jose Dolan met in 1920 had untreatable tuberculosis, an 8th grade education, no money, and a sketchy job history. Eleven years later, Lillian Hellman met Hollywood's wealthy and famous man of the hour, whose TB was in permanent remission. (Granger, NYC)

Lillian Hellman, 1941.
Her *Watch on the Rhine*
opened on Broadway and
Hammett wrote the
screenplay for the film
version. They were civil
rights activists together, and,
despite absences and
infidelities, loved each other
until Hammett died 20 years
later. (Photofest)

Cissy Pascal, 1913, the
year Raymond Chandler met
her. She was a showy
redhead, she was fun, and she
was happy. He got the idea
that he couldn't fail her.
(UCLA Library Special
Collections, Charles E. Young
Research Library)

Raymond Chandler, 1918. He was 30, in love with a married woman, and supporting his mother with whom he lived. Chandler escaped into the Canadian Army. (Mina Whiting/UCLA Library Special Collections, Charles E. Young Research Library)

Raymond Chandler, 1939, the year of his breakthrough novel, *The Big Sleep*. Chandler was 51. Cissy was 69, always sick, and didn't like her husband's first novel or any of those that followed. (Photofest)

Raymond Chandler, c. 1947. Los Angeles's knight errant scowls on one of its beaches in a photograph for *Condé Nast*. (George Platt Lynes/*Condé Nast* Archive/CORBIS)

Kenneth Millar, c. 1921, in Kitchener, Ontario, walled in by dour
adult relatives, including his mother, far right. He felt guilty in the face
of circumstances he could not possibly have been responsible for, much
less controlled. (Mary V. Carr/Courtesy of Tom Nolan)

The Millar Family, 1948, on a trip home to
Kitchener. Margaret Millar was already a popular
mystery writer. Her husband Ken (pen name Ross
Macdonald), with two minor books published, was
trying to play his wife's game. Their daughter Linda
was nine years old. (University of Waterloo Library)

Eudora Welty, c. 1970s. A chance meeting in the lobby of the Algonquin Hotel in 1971 expanded into the easiest, healthiest, romantic relationship Macdonald ever had. As for Welty, he was the love of her life. (Photofest)

Ross Macdonald, 1975. His later, best novels made him a man at the far side of pain. He had written himself well—or well enough. (Photofest)

Chapter Four

Sons and Ghosts

In a lifetime there are myriad refused lovers who become ghosts. Societies have their prohibitions, and in the American days of Hammett and Chandler, homosexuality was illegal, unnatural, and not discussed. Remember that, according to Freud, humanity's basic unit is not the single person but that person's family; thus, what that family thinks about homosexuality matters to that gay individual, who is checking his impulses and staying in the closet, internalizing the taboo and hence loathing that aspect of himself that his family and community hates.

It was a little easier for Macdonald: he was a generation younger than Hammett and Chandler and he agreed with Freud's thinking on sexuality. That Macdonald's lover was a woman makes sense for his orientation later in life. Yet for all Macdonald's courage as a confessional writer, he only briefly admitted to homosexuality and barely acknowledged his suicide attempt in "Notes of a Son and Father." Certainly, he never circled back to either subject, nor did they appear more than fleetingly in his fiction. The number of gay men in Macdonald's work probably can be counted on one hand. And what happened to the pattern of homosexuality in Macdonald's youth? He gained self-control over the behavior and then it stopped. What apparently troubled him most was his bullying of other boys and taking sexual advantage of a retarded maid more than once. Still, this was a frequently occurring, urgent-feeling activity and yet Macdonald didn't elaborate.

It's useful to know what the thinking on sexual orientation was in the 1950s when Macdonald began analysis. Freud's "inversion theory" postulates that all babies are born bisexuals and then influenced by biological and environmental factors in their early childhoods eventually to become predominantly homosexual or heterosexual. William Masters, of Masters and Johnson renown, building on the findings of Freud and Alfred Kinsey, believed that

> [w]e are not genetically determined to be homosexual and we are not genetically determined to be heterosexual. We are born man and woman and sexual beings. We learn sex preferences and our orientations, be it homosexual, heterosexual, bisexual, and, not infrequently, we change voluntarily our sexual preference.[1]

Macdonald appears to have shared similar views. "For whatever else he may be"—says Edward Margolies in his study of the private eye in Hammett, Chandler, Macdonald, and Chester Himes—"Macdonald is a child of the post-World War II neo-Freudian zeitgeist that has posited that human beings of either sex are composites of so-called masculine and feminine traits."[2] Sexual orientation, then, is a continuum. Being bisexual, or owning up to having homosexual experiences in his youth, may have been a label with which Macdonald could live.

Maybe Raymond Chandler could too, but very privately. In just one letter, Chandler talked about bisexuality as "a matter of time and custom."[3] If he was bisexual or homosexual, he was fully engaged in repression as a defense mechanism against lifelong anxiety. Michael Kahn outlines the underlying mindset of that repression:

The erotic desire for a forbidden person is dangerous. If the person I desire is . . . a person of my gender, being aware of that desire would put me in danger of painful guilt feelings. Were I to disclose the desire I would be in further danger, that of being shamed or punished. If I am aware of the impulse and manage to keep it entirely hidden, I must deal not only with the guilt but also with the frustration of a strong need that can never be satisfied. It seems clearly to my advantage *not* to be aware of the desire.[4]

Is Marlowe gay? Chandler doesn't mean for him to be, yet Marlowe delivers erotic descriptions of men—for instance, gushing when he describes Red Norgaard in *Farewell, My Lovely*:

His voice was soft, dreamy, so delicate for a big man that it was startling. It made me think of another soft-voiced big man I had strangely liked. . . . He had the eyes you never see, that you only read about. Violet eyes. Almost purple. Eyes like a girl, a lovely girl. His skin was as soft as silk. Lightly reddened, but it would never tan. It was too delicate. . . . His hair was that shade of red that glints with gold.[5]

The details Chandler uses to describe Chris Lavery in *The Lady in the Lake* are in that same vein:

He had everything in the way of good looks the snapshot had indicated. He had a terrific torso and magnificent thighs. His eyes were chestnut brown and the whites of them slightly gray-white. His hair was rather long and curled a little over his temples. His brown skin showed no signs of dissipation. He was a nice piece of beef.[6]

In 1950 Chandler was commissioned by director Alfred Hitchcock to write the screenplay for Patricia Highsmith's novel *Strangers on a Train.* Hitchcock came daily to check on Chandler's progress, and they drove each other nuts. Donald Spoto wrote about Hitchcock's own "inner experience of division" and suggests that the two men "were surprisingly similar; the tension between them derived not from a confrontation between complementary talents, but from a smoldering suspicion that each knew the other's soul rather more fully than either desired."[7] Certainly, Highsmith's book is all about doubleness and duplicity, as the following passage signals.

> Each was what the other had not chosen to be, the cast-off self, what he thought he hated but perhaps in reality loved. ... there was that duality permeating nature. ... Two people in each person. There's also a person exactly the opposite of you, somewhere in the world, and he waits in ambush.[8]

The finished movie starring Robert Walker and Farley Granger added its own secrets. Patrick McGillian, another Hitchcock biographer, explains that

> [t]he director got Walker; the studio got Granger—but Granger's casting changed a key idea of Hitchcock's. Bruno's homosexuality is implied in the script, but there's no question of Guy's heterosexuality; he's in the middle of a messy divorce and has a girlfriend. ... But as it was, the director had to accept an odd crisscross in the casting: a straight actor (Robert Wagner) playing a homosexual, who comes on to a "super straight" (to borrow Robert L. Carringer's word) played by a homosexual (Granger).[9]

Hitchcock later said that the casting saved him a reel's worth of storytelling because audiences would sense hidden qualities in the actors that wouldn't need to be spelled out. There is available now a prerelease British print of *Strangers on a Train* in which Bruno is flamboyantly attracted to Guy.

The *Long Goodbye* is Chandler's last solid fiction and his most honest. "I wrote this as I wanted to because I can do that now," he said.[10] It includes the self-loathing suicide note of Roger Wade, a novelist: "I was lying like that once in bed and the dark animal was doing it to me, bumping himself against the underside of the bed, and I had an orgasm. That disgusted me more than any other of the nasty things I have done."[11] The more crucial relationship is Marlowe's with Terry Lennox, a drunk with Chandler's war experience whom Marlowe helps get to Mexico when Sylvia Lennox is murdered. Safely there, Lennox writes to Marlowe in farewell:

> So forget it and me. But first drink a gimlet for me at Victor's. And the next time you make coffee, pour me a cup and put some bourbon in and light me a cigarette and put it beside the cup. And after that forget the whole thing. Terry Lennox over and out. And so goodbye.[12]

Marlowe finally beds a woman and gets a marriage proposal from Linda Loring, but he demurs. That scene, however, is not the long goodbye. Afterward Marlowe goes to see Lennox one more time, telling him, "It was nice while it lasted. So long, amigo. I won't say goodbye. I said it to you when it meant something. I said it when it was sad and lonely and final."[13] And that's the long goodbye.

In his introduction to *Trouble Is My Business*, Chandler writes: "The fictional detective is a catalyst, not a Casanova."[14] In *The Long Goodbye*, Marlowe is inarguably more Casanova than catalyst, with the argument being, whom does he love?

Chandler is at pains to make Marlowe homophobic: for example, in *The Big Sleep* he has him brag: "I took plenty of the punch. It was meant to be a hard one, but a pansy has no iron in his bones, whatever he looks like."[15] Openly gay men are repeatedly the victims of sadistic brutality: to wit, Marlowe's "butchering of the homosexual youth, Carol Lundgren, in *The Big Sleep*"[16] and, in *Farewell, My Lovely*, Mrs. Grayle's pounding "Lindsay Marriott's head until he has 'brains on his face.'"[17] Stephen Knight states, "As far as men go, Marlowe is very hostile if they are effeminate."

> Arthur Geiger in *The Big Sleep* and Lindsay Marriott in *Farewell, My Lovely* are clearly homosexual and they both die grotesquely, immediately after being examined with disfavour by Marlowe. Intriguingly, he also disliked men who are fully dependent on women, gigolos such as Chris Lavery in *The Lady in the Lake* and Louis Vannier in *The High Window*. They also die in ugly ways. Evidently feminine power over men is not enjoyed at all, and sexual unease comes strongly through all Marlowe's encounters with men and women. None of these feelings, it is interesting to notice, is in the least related to the unveiling of urban corruption.[18]

The man who wrote Marlowe may have needed to insist that he was like Marlowe. Without doubt, Chandler was an unapologetic homophobe too:

> [P]ansies, queers, homos, whatever you want to call them. . . . These are sick people who try to conceal their sickness. My reaction may be uncharitable: they just make me sick. My dead wife could spot one entering a room. Highly sexed women invariably seem to have that reaction.[19]

Chandler was given to blustering heterosexual bravado, telling a friend in 1956, "The most strict and puritanical woman I had ever met had been in bed with me a week after I met her,"[20] and informing another friend in 1957, "Thank God I can still copulate like a thirty-year-old."[21]

One of Chandler's doublenesses was that he was both an Englishman and an American. There were ramifications beyond geography: in the United States, he was professionally regarded as an adept, popular, genre writer; in England, he was lionized as a mainstream, literary novelist. In the United States he was considered to be heterosexual but, within his circle of English friends, the usual assumption was that he was in the closet. Patricia Highsmith said, "Maleness sat uneasily on him."[22]

"The English public school system had left its sexually devastating mark upon him," John Houseman commented. He, likewise a graduate of that same system, thought Chandler was "too inhibited to be [outwardly] gay."[23] Natasha Spender—who was Chandler's friend in his last years and whose husband, Stephen Spender, was bisexual—remembers in her essay, "His Own Long Goodbye," that "we all, without a second thought, assumed that he was a repressed homosexual."

> His mother had divorced his drunken and violent father, taking her seven-year-old son to England to live with her mother and sister in Dulwich—in a middle-class household of high Victorian rectitude.
>
> . . . Raymond always talked of his own schooldays at Dulwich College with pride . . . for his character of exceptional sexual purity. . . . Clinically this pattern of childhood situations is often recognized as a determining factor for later homosexuality.[24]

Upon hearing that Chandler had claimed, yet again, "My wife hated them [homosexuals] and she could spot one just by walking into a room,"[25] Don Bachardy, Christopher Isherwood's lover, remarked:

"Well, it's perfect, isn't it? He married his mother. A woman who hated queers. It's the perfect cover. How much more protective can you get?"[26]

Yet Chandler incontrovertibly loved his wife. He had bought her the house in La Jolla in 1946, and in 1952, when Cissy was eighty-two and very sick and they had been recluses for years, they took a trip to England and New York City. He wanted to show her where he had come of age and to see where she did. That is more than reverence; that is curiosity born of wanting to understand and be understood better. "She was the beat of my heart for thirty years. She was the music I heard faintly at the edge of sound,"[27] he wrote at the time she died. Dilys Powell, the film critic of the *Sunday Times*, and her husband, Leonard Russell, literary editor of the same newspaper, had had a dinner for the Chandlers. In a gentle essay written after their deaths, "Ray and Cissy," Powell remembers her first impressions:

> Looking back now, I realize that, leaving aside the brilliant literary gifts which first seduced me, I liked Raymond best in his relationship with Cissy, that smiling propitiatory figure whom he guarded and defended. . . . In a world with Cissy he showed another kind of gallantry; he shielded her.[28]

If gay was Chandler's place on the continuum, then the sexually knowing and sophisticated Cissy would have figured that out somewhere in the years of their marriage. She may have accepted her husband's complete nature, even as he forgave her own lie; they may have protected each other's secrets. As Wyatt indicates: "If the novels were a product of the marriage, they grew out of its darkness and secrets as well as its love. Love and marriage become, in Chandler's novels, the site of secrecy itself."[29] Maybe the story of Cissy and Chandler's marriage is as simple and complicated as this: that they came to love, forgive, and shield each other.

W eakening a societal taboo is like turning a barge—it takes a
long time. But it happens: it's easier to be gay today than in
Chandler and even Macdonald's time. Incest, however, long has
been held abominable, and psychoanalytic thinking about it has not
changed in the 102 years since Freud wrote *Totem and Taboo*,
wherein incest and patricide are the two practices held incompatible
with the very definition of civilization. Yet the ghost lovers are there.

The Electra complex, as formulated by Freud and used in psychoanalysis in the 1950s in the United States, is axiomatic in the sexual
development of girls. Its stages parallel the Oedipus complex and
begin with a little girl's attraction to her mother. Soon, though, she
comes to believe that her mother already has castrated her and therefore the child turns against her, becoming libidinously attracted to
her father and fantasizing about being impregnated by him. In a
later stage achieved if all goes well, the complex is successfully
resolved: the girl, not wanting to give up her mother's love, allows
her hostility to ease; in fact, she both "internalizes" her mother and
becomes attracted to other, appropriate males. But things don't
always go well: "The mother may simply lose interest in the father,"
Michael Kahn summarizes,

> and send the message that she would like the daughter to
> take over for her.
> [U]nconsciously the daughter passionately desires the
> victory. That is the reason the victory is so terribly costly. We
> recall once again that in the realm of primary process the
> wish is equivalent to the act: "I wanted to take him away from
> her and I have done it." Now the daughter unconsciously
> believes that she has willfully committed what may be the
> two most terrible sins: incest and matricide. She is certainly

better off if the incest has only been symbolic, but psychic
incest and matricide it is nevertheless, making her prey to
consuming guilt.[30]

Eleven-year-old Linda Millar wanted to go with her dad to Ann
Arbor for the summer of 1952, just the two of them. She would, she
said, "keep house" for him. "This in spite of a long history of what
can only be described as emotional neglect where it counted most,
an inability to love enough, to father his own flesh," Macdonald
sadly writes in "Notes of a Son and Father."

Macdonald turned Linda down and went alone to the University
of Michigan. When he came back home in August, he

> found wife and child in a bad way, and "attempted suicide."
> The wife . . . suggested that he should have himself committed,
> but nothing was done. The husband resisted any thought of
> help, and is not sorry, except for the child's sake. [31]

When Macdonald was twelve, his father had invited him to come
along on a last, West-wandering adventure, and the boy had turned
him down. It was at about that same time that Macdonald stopped
sleeping in his mother's bed and that she talked to him about her
marriage, referring to "'incompatibility' with sexual implications."[32]
Thereafter, the almost-adolescent boy's anger ratcheted up.

When sixteen-year-old Linda drank two quarts of wine and
started driving, the dynamic equation of Macdonald, Margaret, and
Linda was sexually precarious. In "Notes of a Son and Father," Macdonald refers to

> the wife's real need for a jealous and exclusive love (the father
> was half her world; the converse is less true) and I think
> hyper-awareness of the fairly normal incestuous content in
> the father-daughter relationship. This has its other side: the

daughter has been perhaps unhealthily aware of her parents' sexual life and jealous of it. But it is hard to know where normality ends.

Shortly thereafter, Macdonald composed an essay, "Memorial Day," which includes this assessment of the family dynamic:

On the eve of Memorial Day, I stared at my wife in helpless pride and longing. . . . She railed at me, saying I was sick, would always be sick. I held myself in silence for the most part, but there was trouble and the shadow of blackmail. Linda slammed a door.[33]

Margaret Millar's canon is full of angry families. In *Beast in View*, the father says to his adolescent daughter, "Your punishment, Helen, is being you and having to live with yourself."[34] The mother in *Vanish in an Instant*, written presciently years before Linda Millar's troubles, has given up:

All my life I've done everything possible for her. She's been hard to raise, terribly hard. It's been one crisis after another ever since the day she was born, and I've met each one with all the strength I had. Now I don't have enough left to go on with. . . . Virginia's on her own now. When she makes a mistake she must correct it herself. I won't be here to help her.[35]

Many of her plots have children overhearing what their parents really think of them or forceful women choosing emotionally weak men.

A different man might have witnessed his adolescent daughter's self-destruction in shocked surprise, but Macdonald admitted recognition; he had been here before. Knowing without knowing gave way to knowingness, and his canon turned a corner.

"Time pressing, time lapsing, time repeating itself in dark acts
. . . is the wicked fairy to troubled people, granting them inevitably the
thing they dread,"[36] writes Welty in her review of *The Underground
Man*. And, more often than not, a child who needs help now is the
emergency that hastens Archer and the reader through Macdonald's
novels. "We find at the center of Ross Macdonald's complicated
novels," George Grella avers in his *New Republic* essay "Evil Plots,"
"as at the center of Dickens' complicated novels, a suffering child."[37]
Paul Nelson concurs:

> Those stories of fractured families, reckless runaways and
> damaged young people who are haunted by eerie, early mem-
> ories that *something* has happened—something terrible, but
> they aren't quite sure what—seemed both jinglingly imme-
> diate and terrifyingly tribal, daring to fiddle with the fuse of
> that timeless bomb within us all, planted somewhere in the
> past and set to go off who knows when.[38]

It took Macdonald five years to write the apology that is *The
Ferguson Affair*. He wanted badly for Santa Barbara to see that the
girl who killed a boy and maimed another was herself wounded by
a malfunctioning childhood not of her own making. The novel's plot
involves both a faked kidnapping wherein a young woman claims
amnesia afterward and a speeding car that causes mortal injury. The
boys whom Linda had run down were Mexicans, and Santa Barbara's
Hispanic community believed there was racism in the light sentence
given to Macdonald's white and comparatively well-to-do daughter.
Macdonald acknowledges the truth of this, having his detective say,
"No one with strong financial backing is ever executed."[39] Reference
is made to there being two towns: "the ambiguous darkness between
two towns, two magics."[40] But the concerns of racism in a small
and wealthy town are in an outer plot inadequately connected to the

underaddressed inner plot of immaturity and personal forgiveness. The novel is sad but not strong, and Macdonald probably knew this, given that he decided to leave Archer out of *The Ferguson Affair* and use Bill Gunnarson instead, and only in this one novel. Nevertheless, its outward reach toward a community of men is the antecedent to two of the best, last Archer novels, *The Underground Man* (1971) and *Sleeping Beauty* (1973).

"[O]ne writes on a curve, on the backs of torn-off calendar sheets," said Macdonald.

A writer in his fifties will not recapture the blaze of youth, or the steadier passion that comes like a second and saner youth in his forties, if he's lucky. But he can lie in wait in his room—it must be at least the hundredth room by now—and keep open his imagination and the bowels of his compassion against the day when another book will haunt him like a ghost rising out of both the past and the future.[41]

Macdonald was right: he had ten more books in him after *The Ferguson Affair*. "He was like a ghost from the past, you know?" says Archer of a character in *Sleeping Beauty*. "A poor little roughed-up hammered-down ghost, . . . that shriveled little throw-away of a man without his clothes."[42] Macdonald's life and work was haunted by his wife, his daughter, his grandson, and himself—all rendered as children in need of good parents—and their real and failed mothers and fathers who were unequal to the task.

Macdonald is able to link the collective unconscious to warnings about our aggregate future in *The Underground Man*. Two cuckolded spouses, for example, become real estate developers, recklessly overbuilding tract housing, thereby "raping" the landscape. Not only is Stanley Broadhurst neglecting his wife and son with his obsessed search for his father, but he also distractedly starts a southern California forest fire, and that too is a kind of murder. Archer hears the fire "breathing," as if it were alive and even somehow human.

Sleeping Beauty focuses on beautiful and missing young Laurel Russo and her parents. "They were one of those couples who don't pull together,"[43] says Archer:

> When there's trouble in a family, it tends to show up in its weakest member. And the other members of the family know that. They make allowances for the one in trouble, try to protect her and so on, because they know they're implicated themselves.[44]

Misplaced guilt has damaged the family's members for generations, now injuring this sad daughter. "He seemed to feel responsible for her death," Archer says of another character, "But he may not have done what he thought he did. Sometimes a man like Nelson feels terribly guilty simply because he's been punished so much."[45] The same family is responsible for a gas spill in 1945 and an oil spill in the novel's present. Remember Michael Kreyling's contention that, in Macdonald's novels, dysfunction in the intimate family pushes outward into the wider arenas of past and future, political and natural worlds. Macdonald considered environmental crimes to be moral ones, and his canon's shift after 1956 from physical to moral engagement made possible twinning familial guilt with ecological culpability. It is an appropriate combination, ecology having to do with the connections of live organisms to one another.

Uncared-for children haunted Macdonald and consistently motivate Archer. Children are rare and unprivileged in Hammett's canon. Hammett didn't put his steady attendance to his children into his fictional families; he used his family-of-origin as a template instead. Jo admitted that "the loving family holding hands . . . had not been his experience. That attitude shows in his work, where families have rapacious mothers, wandering daughters, even fathers who kill their sons."[46] True enough, but the more glaring proof is that the combined number of mothers and fathers of little children in all his fiction is so low. One would need to go back to "Don Key" to find one.

Yet "a child who needs help now" was the circumstance that had precipitated Hammett's marriage in 1921 and seemed to repeat itself during an anomalous few months in 1937. Hellman told Hammett she was pregnant and demanded that he divorce Jose after all those years and marry her. Hellman must have known that a baby was the one argument for marriage that would work with both Hammett and Jose. So he did it: he showed up at Jose's house in Santa Monica with papers and, after hushed conversation, Jose signed them.[47] They had a Mexican divorce with no standing in the United States, something Hammett knew and Jose found comfort in. Jose was the little girl who had been a surrendered child and was now a surrendered wife. Hammett—the man who had married a pregnant nurse—was now prepared to marry a pregnant playwright. Hellman subsequently and unilaterally decided to get an abortion. Marriage between Hammett and herself apparently never was mentioned again.[48]

His daughters drove much of the best of Hammett's biography: the proof is in how much effortful time he spent with them, in his (posthumously published) letters to them and to Jose about them, and in his long attempt to live with Mary and find her help. After Jose and Hammett's tacit separation in 1929, the man-about-town saw his children once or twice a week in San Francisco and later brought them to Hollywood and New York City for lengthy visits. Jo remembered baking lemon pies and bread with her dad, his making soap pictures on mirrors and little books of drawings and poetry for them, his taking Mary "to the fights at the old Olympic Gardens and [her] to the races at Santa Anita."[49] Hammett wrote Jo from the

Aleutian Islands on her birthday: "So now you're eighteen and I'm all out of child daughters. My family is cluttered up with grown women. There's nobody who has to say, 'Sir,' to me and there are no more noses to wipe."[50] In 1948 Jo got engaged and wrote Hammett asking if he would give her away. He wrote right back, "Give you away? Why I'll drop you like a hot potato!"[51] When Jo had children, Hammett was a joyful grandpa, once taking a one-year-old granddaughter by himself across country by plane.

They wooed their father differently, these Hammett Electras. Hammett got his young daughters subscriptions to the *New Yorker* and *New Masses*; they would pore over "Talk of the Town" because it felt sophisticated in the same way their dad was, and Mary especially would come up with political questions that Hammett carefully answered. "Be in favor of what's good for the workers and against what isn't,"[52] he told her. He would write to his elder daughter about politics for the rest of his life.

But, as they grew, Jo was still easy to love; Mary wasn't, and Hammett loved her anyway. Hammett had told them that he "admired people who went too far"[53]; maybe Mary was aiming to do that. Jo remembered her big sister throwing their mother's nursing mementos in the gutter and "slugging a nun at the Catholic school."[54]

> She grew into a beautiful girl—Lillian said that at sixteen she was one of the most beautiful she had ever seen—and the house was always full of boys. In the beginning they were neighborhood kids, but soon they became older and more scary. . . . Her drinking started early, and by fourteen she was a full-blown alcoholic. Later there were pills.[55]

Mary was nineteen when she and Jo went to New York again to stay with their father for a month. Mary boasted to Hammett about her sexual abandon. "I learned later," Jo said, that she had told him all about herself and men. I imagine she sort of bragged about it, thinking he'd understand, admire her daring and to-hell-with-bourgeoisie spirit. Of course, he didn't. He was terribly hurt. What she never understood was that although he might have lived that kind of life himself, he never approved of it, even for himself, and certainly not for his daughter.[56]

"We carry invisible templates as ineluctably ourselves as finger-prints," writes Doris Lessing, "but we don't know about them until we look around us and see them mirrored."[57]

At twenty-four Mary was worse. Jose did what she never did and asked Hammett to come and help. Hammett took Mary with him to New York and got her psychiatric help. She lived with her father intermittently for five years but didn't get better. Then she came home to Jose permanently. After Mary married feckless Kenny Miller, she and he both lived with Jose. When I asked Jo's daughter, Julie Marshall Rivett, why her grandmother didn't make a new life for herself after Hammett, she said simply, "There was always Mary." Rivett added, "I wonder what Mary would be diagnosed with today."[58] Mary died undiagnosed, obese and vengeful in a nursing home in 1992.

Chapter Five
After the Books

"Addiction grows in the dark places created by secrets," writes John Cheever's daughter in *Desire: Where Sex Meets Addiction*. She goes on to say:

> There are many causes, of course: there is brain chemistry and genetic predisposition, and there is character and opportunity. Most of all, there are secrets and fakery, worlds created to mask the real world and images meant to fool everyone. Addicts are brilliant storytellers, and my father was one of the best.[1]

Chandler told stories too. Here is a doctor in his Hollywood novel, *The Little Sister*:

> [A]ll the little neurotic types that can't take it cold. Have to have their little pills and little shots in the arm. Have to have help over the humps. It gets to be all humps after a while. ... They can be deprived of their drug. Eventually after great suffering they can do without it. That is not curing them, my

friend. That is not removing the nervous or emotional flaw
which made them become addicts. It is making them dull
negative people who sit in the sun and twirl their thumbs and
die of sheer boredom and inanition. . . . A hopeless alcoholic.
You probably know how they are. They drink and drink and
don't eat. And little by little the vitamin deficiency brings
on the symptoms of delirium. There is only one thing to do for
them . . . needles and more needles. . . . I practice among
dirty little people in a dirty little town.²

Chandler was an alcoholic and he died denying it, maybe because
it gave him common ground with his father and that was something
he couldn't think about. In any event, in his oil-business years,
Chandler made lame excuses; during his Hollywood tenure, he gave
unlikely explanations; and as a widower, he told unbelievable stories
that eventually became self-delusional.

In 1946 Cissy and Raymond did two things for the first time:
they moved away from Los Angeles (to La Jolla) and they bought a
house. Artistically, this last move was a mistake; Chandler's Los
Angeles is, in significant part, a fiction of place:

I know now what is the matter with my writing or not writing.
. . . Los Angeles is no longer my city. . . . There's nothing for
me to write about. To write about a place you have to love it
or hate it or do both by turns. . . . But a sense of vacuity and
boredom—that is fatal.³

Socializing was tense: Cissy fussed, and Chandler was anxious. It
was easier not to try. A schedule was reassuring: Chandler dressed
every day in a shirt and tie, tried to write in the mornings, had lunch
at home with Cissy, then drove into La Jolla to run his errands.
Chandler liked this, chatting with the lady at the post office, nobody getting too close. Cissy insisted on tea at 4:00 p.m., and they

ate dinner at home because they were hard to please when it came to food. Cissy went to bed early: breathing made her tired, and the medicines made her vague. And so Chandler started writing letters. Although he wrote mostly to his agents, publishers, editors, critics, and other writers—including J. B. Priestly, Somerset Maugham, and S. J. Perelman—the business at hand was just his starting-off point. Taken together, the letters fed Chandler's need to be creative and constitute nearly a writer's notebook and certainly a valuable self-assessment of his canon. Cissy, the post office lady, and the letters: life could be lived, it seemed, safely at a remove.

"In all addictions," claims Susan Cheever, "there is a rupturing of the individual's connection to society—a breaking of the social contract, the divorce of a single man or woman from the human race. . . . An addict is a community of one."[4] But not Chandler: he had Cissy, and they became recluses together—a community of two.

In December 1954 Cissy died; she was eighty-four, but the death certificate reads sixty-eight. She had been married to Chandler for nearly thirty-one years and lived in thirty-five different apartments and rental houses in Los Angeles. Eight people came to her funeral. Chandler was lost, threatening suicide and claiming, "I never wrote anything . . . that I could dedicate to her. I planned it. I thought of it, but I never wrote it. Perhaps I couldn't have written it."[5]

And so Chandler began his own dying, still casting about for extenuated explanations in a letter to Jessica Tyndale, a New York friend and banker, in 1955:

Anyone who can drink a great deal steadily over a long period of time is apt to think of himself as an alcoholic, because liquor is part of his life and he is terribly let down without it. Yet he is not an alcoholic. . . . I said: "Doctor, am I an alcoholic? They told me I was in New York." He said: "If you can become a controlled drinker, and personally I think you can with the right sort of life, you are not an alcoholic."[6]

In 1956, again corresponding with Tyndale, he returned to the topic:

> Finally the head guy said: "You think you are depressed, but
> you are quite wrong. You are a fully integrated personality
> and [I] wouldn't dream of trying to interfere with it by psycho-
> analysis or anything of that sort. All that's the matter with
> you is loneliness. You simply cannot and must not live alone.
> If you do you will inevitably drink and that will make you
> sick."[7]

In February 1955, Chandler shot off his revolver into the bathroom ceiling. He was committed to the local hospital's psychiatric
ward and then moved to a private "drying-out" facility. He checked
himself out against doctors' orders. In March he sold his house and
in April took the train to New York, en route to England. While in
New York, he was hospitalized for alcoholism. Back in his hotel, he
called his secretary in California to tell her he was going to jump out
the window. He did not. He went to England.

Chandler talked incessantly about Cissy in naked, runaway monologues that embarrassed his listeners. His letters were fulsome. Below
are excerpts from three different letters in which he extolled her.

> My sister-in-law says I was the most wonderful husband a
> woman ever had. But isn't it easy to be a wonderful husband
> if you have a wonderful wife?[8]
> But if you find an ideal and an inspiration, you don't cheapen it.[9]
> I wasn't faithful to my wife out of principle but because she
> was completely adorable. . . . I already had perfection.[10]

In London, Natasha Spender organized a "shuttle service" of
women friends to take him to lunch, listen to him, and coax him not
to drink so much. It wasn't easy. Chandler misconstrued the women's

genuine affection for him as sexual. He sent sprays of orchids. He bought them expensive jewelry that they had to refuse diplomatically. He called them after midnight, subjecting the women of the shuttle service to long, lugubrious monologues hinting at suicide.

He was literally hell-bent on finding a new woman in need of rescue, someone stricken whom he could marry. The women he found weren't all as kind as those in the shuttle service. After drying out yet again in New York and La Jolla, Chandler went to San Francisco to meet a woman who had written him after one of his suicide attempts. Chandler already loved her, he was convinced, and he had changed his will and was planning a wedding. It took one weekend together to end things. There would be another, similar woman who would take advantage of him and tell him about her divorce problems; he, in turn, would give her too much of his money and dignity.

Overlapping and nearly outlasting that mess was Helga Greene, Chandler's English literary agent—an able, efficient, single, and self-supporting soul. With her substantive encouragement, Chandler wrote a last novel, the only one he wrote while drinking. In *Playback*, Marlowe is weary:

> Give up? Sure I give up. I'm in the wrong business. I ought to have given up before I started. All you get out of this racket is problems you can't solve, clients who beat you out of your fees, people you don't want to know, and cracks on the noggin that make you punchy as a stand-by prelim fighter who gets fifty bucks to wait in a cold dressing room with broken hands and a face full of scar tissue in case the main event ends too quick to give the customers their bucket of blood. The hell with it.[11]

Greene grew worried about Chandler and agreed to marry him; that way he could live permanently in England with her and get free medical care. In a bizarre scene in New York, Chandler insisted upon asking Greene's father for her hand in marriage. H. S. H. Guinness was disinclined to encourage his daughter to marry a seventy-year-old groom with significant problems. Chandler acquiesced. He and Greene would have to wait for Guinness to die. So, Chandler didn't go to England and didn't marry Greene. Instead, he went back to La Jolla, lived alone for three weeks, drank heavily, and died on March 26, 1959.

Afterward, Jon Tuska, who writes about film noir, set out to interview people who had known Raymond Chandler. "No one I have spoken with who knew [him] has the foggiest notion of what he wanted from life,"[12] Tuska subsequently reported. "He was a chronically unhappy man,"[13] wrote George V. Higgins. "Nobody understands me," Philip Marlowe says, "I'm enigmatic."[14]

Hammett became a drunk—and a mean one—after leaving Jose. In 1932 Elise De Viane, a "starlet," sued Hammett for sexual assault and battery, and she won a $2,500 judgment. He used a friend as go-between to give money to a different woman "in trouble." His venereal disease recurred.

At a party, Hammett was seated next to a formerly well-known actress who had aged beyond the roles for which she was famous.

> During the meal, tomato sauce spilled on her beige dress and Hammett boomed, "Doesn't it remind you of when we were both still menstruating?"[15]

Years later, when Mary came east to live with her father, they drank together and there was a rumor that he slapped her around. His other daughter, Jo, writes that alcohol made

my father . . . sarcastic-mean. . . . drunk he had a kind of
lashing-out desperation about him that scared me to death.
I couldn't understand how anyone so funny and kind could
turn so awful; why a man who cared for his privacy and dignity
so much could trash them.[16]

Most of what Hammett did when he was drunk seemed unleashed:
anger, threatened physical violence against men and mostly verbal
violence against women. In his unfinished and posthumously published novel *Tulip*, the eponymous character says, "It wasn't so
much that I was quarrelsome when I drank as that I forgot not to
be."[17] Hammett was a famously, remarkably "unangry" man when he
was sober. Maybe while sober, he could control the rage he really
felt and when he was drunk, the anger broke out, unrestrained.

Alcoholism wrecked Hammett's writing career. His last Op story
was published in 1930, and he couldn't write reviews for the *Saturday
Review of Literature* anymore—a job he had taken pride in. Except for
Watch on the Rhine, he never made much of a go of screenwriting.

But he wrote *The Thin Man*, published in 1934. Dedicated "To
Lillian Hellman," it was his last, saddest novel, although it made
Hammett wealthy. It is two leveled, in the same way that Hammett's
frantic spending on starlets, hotel suites, expensive eating and drinking, and incautious generosity to strangers and drinking friends was
sophisticated, arch, and glamorous on its surface with distraught
dissipation at its root. It says something about the American reader
during the Depression and about what one expects to find when
reading a detective story that *The Thin Man* was a huge hit as a mad-
cap comedy. Detective fiction writer Donald Westlake did recognize
The Thin Man's double structure:

When I was fourteen or fifteen I read Hammett's *The Thin Man*
(the first Hammett I'd read) and it was a defining moment. It

was a sad, lonely, lost book, that pretended to be cheerful
and aware and full of good fellowship, and I hadn't known
you could do that: seem to be telling this, but really tell
that; three-dimensional writing, like three-dimensional
chess.[18]

The novel is a cautionary tale: retirement is dangerous. Nick
Charles has been retired for six years. All the suspects come to him
in *The Thin Man*, and the minimal hard-boiled thinking he does is
spaced between drinking, flirting with women, and being witty. In
Hammett's 1924 short story "The Scorched Face," a cop named Pat
Reddy has married a rich wife but refuses the chance to change
his life. The Op comments approvingly: "I don't know what his wife
did with her money, but Pat didn't even improve the quality of his
cigars—though he should have."[19] Now, ten years later, here is
Charles living off his wife. Critic and poet John Irwin realized an
interesting connection:

> It seems only appropriate that Hammett's last novel was pub-
> lished in the same year, 1934, as Fitzgerald's *Tender Is the
> Night*, and the structural resemblance between the two books
> is noteworthy—each is the story of a man who marries an
> heiress and of the effect the wife's money has on his career.[20]

The Thin Man is facile: if everyone is amusing all the time, maybe
they don't have to admit to despair. The novel ends with Nick and
Nora Charles doing just that:

> "This excitement has put us all behind in our drinking."
> "It's all right by me. What do you think will happen to Mimi
>   and Gilbert now?"
> "Nothing new. They'll go on being Mimi and Dorothy and Gilbert
>   just as you and I will go on being us and the Quinns will go

> on being the Quinns. Murder doesn't round out anybody's
> life except the murdered's and sometimes the murderer's."
"That may be," Nora said, "but it's all pretty unsatisfactory."[21]

In 1948, a doctor told Hammett he would die if he continued drinking and so, in a very Op or Spade-like move, he quietly quit for good.

"It would be good to say that as his life changed the productivity increased, but it didn't," Hellman said afterward. "Perhaps the vigor and the force had dissipated."[22] Soon Hammett was referring to "reformed drunks who 'should have stayed drunk, so that they don't wake up to find out they haven't any talent.'"[23]

But what is the real answer? Why did Hammett stop writing? There are three answers—or approaches to three answers. First, he did other things instead. He lost years to alcoholism and lung cancer at the end. He found that he liked teaching and was good at it. He began by substantively mentoring Hellman. He found her a true story about a disturbed girl in a Scottish boarding school conjuring up an accusation of lesbianism against two of her teachers. He then coached Hellman, painstakingly vetting and exhorting, and the result was *The Children's Hour*. The man who girded himself against revealed introspection drove Hellman to write about her mother and her mother's family in *The Little Foxes*, a second critical success. Years later a friend suggested to Hellman that she needn't put up with Hammett's drunkenness. Hellman replied, "You don't understand. He gave me *The Little Foxes*."[24] In 1943 Hammett won the Oscar for Best Screenplay of Hellman's *Watch on the Rhine*.

Hammett flabbergasted everybody, including the US Army, by successfully enlisting in World War II. He was forty-eight, with bum lungs and a membership in the American Communist Party. The military sent him to bleak Adak, one of the Aleutian Islands, where he created a camp newspaper. Hammett had a ball: he got Jose to send him wool socks and Lillian to send him news clippings daily.

He wrote controversial editorials—"Don't Let 'Em Kid You into Buying War Bonds"[25] was one. Even better, he taught his young staff of GIs, who called him "Pop," how to be journalists. William Marling, who writes about Hammett and Chandler, thinks that

> the Army provided Hammett with an opportunity: service was patriotic, it was a political statement, it removed him from the Los Angeles-New York circuit, and allowed him to practice the egalitarianism that he preached. He probably suspected that the structured environment, and the calm spaces it afforded, allowed him to compose a new Dashiell Hammett to meet the world.[26]

"Maybe a life ruled over by other people solved some of the problems,"[27] said Hellman.

Or maybe living and working only with men, as Hammett had done as a happy Pinkerton, was easier. Not so surprisingly, he later kind of liked prison. The man who said "I like women, I really like women"[28] and who literally had them crossing each other on the stairs may have felt off balance in their company.

After the war and later after jail, Hammett taught at the Marxist Jefferson School of Social Science in lower Manhattan. His course, Mystery Writing, was billed as "devoted to the history of the mystery story, the relationship between the detective story and the general novel, and the possibility of the detective story as a progressive medium in literature."[29] A student remembers, "He taught us that tempo is the vital thing in fiction, that you've got to keep things moving, and that character can be drawn *within* the action. . . . He was very serious, very intense when he talked about writing."[30]

Hammett was a nonviolent Marxist who loved his country and had no interest in visiting, much less championing, communist countries. His views that were communist in 1937 are still around and merely liberal in 2015: voting rights for blacks and other minorities, pro-

union, immigration for victims of political persecution in their home-
lands, and the right of federal and state employees to voice their
political beliefs without reprisal. Hammett worked at his politics,
assuming offices in, signing petitions for, endorsing public letters
from, acting as spokesman for, and donating money and services to
myriad leftist organizations.

Hammett was one of three trustees of the Civil Rights Congress's
(CRC) bail fund, which was used to bail out persons arrested for
political reasons. The fund's contributors were kept secret. In 1949
the CRC bailed out eleven men convicted under the Smith Act of
"criminal conspiracy to teach and advocate the overthrow of the
United States by force and violence." Four of the eleven men jumped
bail. The US District Court, Southern District of New York, sub-
poenaed the three trustees, wanting to know where the four fugitives
were and who the bail contributors were. On July 9, 1951, Hammett
appeared in District Court and refused to answer questions. Finding
Hammett guilty of contempt of court, the judge asked him if he had
anything to say before being sentenced. He said peaceably, "Not a
thing," and went off to federal prison for six months.[31] Hellman later
said that "he talked about going to jail the way people talk about
going to college."[32] In 1957 journalist James Cooper asked Hammett
why hadn't written while in prison. Hammett said, "I was never bored
enough."[33]

A second approach to why Hammett stopped writing is to look
at the nature and path of the writing he had done. *Red Harvest* and
The Maltese Falcon are Hammett's best novels and are more hard-
boiled than his other three—that is, they operate within more of the
hard-boiled conventions. Hammett was in a frustrating situation: he
wanted to break out of the hard-boiled genre and write serious,
mainstream novels, yet the further his work got from being hard-
boiled, the less critically successful it was.

Beginning in 1926, Hammett wrote longer hard-boiled fiction.
Both he and Shaw believed that was the direction in which to go. Yet

the detectives in Hammett's novels are "softer" than those in his stories, which is to say, more fleshed out. It could be said that when the detectives acquired human weaknesses, they stopped being hard-boiled. It is true that the trajectory from the Op to Spade to Beaumont to Charles is in the direction of no detective at all. But the latter two characters aren't less hard-boiled because they have depth and flaws. The are less hard-boiled because they make no attempt to resist checking their worst impulses, in part because they lack or have abrogated a personal value system, a code. All of this is to say that Hammett could—and did in *Red Harvest* and *The Maltese Falcon*—create *human* hard-boiled detectives.

Consider too a possible working definition of hard-boiled fiction: an existential man in a nihilistic world. *Black Mask* historian Herbert Ruhm points out, "The left-wing periodicals of the Thirties had given Hammett no play . . . perhaps because his work suggests no solution: no mass-action . . . no Emersonian reconciliation and transcendence."[34]

In the 1930s, Hammett's politics made him more hopeful about the world. As an active Marxist and a humanistic philosopher, Hammett came to believe in a different worldview: man can effect change for the good. Sinda Gregory thinks that

> [a]s a Marxist, he believed in the pursuit of economic and personal freedom; a cohesive, meaningful world was possible and all his political efforts worked towards that end. . . . He was carried by his fiction to an aesthetic and philosophical position that *is* chaos and random transformation. . . . Thus his deeply-felt political convictions clashed with his artistic beliefs.[35]

In his introduction to a collection of Op pieces, Steven Marcus elaborates on the same insight:

His creative career ends when he is no longer able to handle the literary, social, and moral opacities, instabilities, and contradictions that characterize all his best work. His life then splits apart and goes in the two opposite directions that were implicit in his earlier, creative phase, but that the creativity held suspended and in poised yet fluid tension. His politics go in one direction; the way he made his living went in another—he became a hack writer, and then finally no writer at all.[36]

Can there be a hard-boiled detective in a world that can be imbued with meaning? He needn't actually make the world better; he just has to believe that he could, that is, believe in the aim and hope. Hammett didn't invent such a man, but Macdonald did—so it can be done. On different paths, Hammett and Macdonald came to a similar place. Through political study and work as an activist, Hammett came to believe that humankind could make the world better. Through Freudian psychoanalysis and work as a writer, Macdonald came to believe that each man can get past primary wounds, which are axiomatically shared, and into a collective, better-but-not-perfect future.

Hammett was famously averse to introspection and, so the theory goes, that is why he couldn't break out of genre work and write mainstream, serious fiction. There is plenty of evidence that he was unwilling or unable to talk about his motivations, fears, and loves, but this doesn't mean he didn't think about these warring forces. Indeed, the proof that he did is in the best of his writing. Through the years of the Op stories and novels, the Op changes, becoming aware of beguiling appetites he is loath to own up to. Hammett could not have written those later Op pieces if he had not experienced that kind of private shame himself. He could not have made *The Thin Man* flamboyant on the surface and depressed beneath if he did not experience his own life at two levels.

Hammett's letters are full of ghosts of books:

> I keep plugging away at the book—which I hope to finish
> next month. . . . I'm trying to get a book—tentatively entitled
> *Man and Boy* started. . . . I was hoping I'd do enough on the
> book to brag about in this space. I did some, but not enough
> to brag about. . . . Not working on it is partly a sort of stage
> fright, I think—putting the finishing touches on a book can
> be kind of frightening.[37]

What the letters and Jo's memoir make plain is that "he didn't
stop writing. Not until the very last. What he stopped was finishing."[38]
That Hammett continued to start for twenty-seven years suggests a
sort of suffering. Anna Freud posits that depression is a defense
mechanism against anxiety, that depression is what people who can't
get angry experience. Perhaps the enraged-when-drunk Hammett
stopped drinking, still couldn't get angry while sober, and got
depressed instead.

When he was dying of lung cancer—not of tuberculosis or alcoholism—Hellman once asked, "Do you want to talk about it?" Hammett
said, "No. My only chance is to not talk about it."[39]

Dashiell Hammett died on January 10, 1961. In his introduction
to *The Continental Op*, Steven Marcus writes, "By his own wish, he
was buried in Arlington National Cemetery. He had served the
nation in two World Wars. He had served it in other ways, which
were his own."[40] His filmmaker friend, Nunnally Johnson, wrote:

> From the day I met Hammett, in the late 20s, his behavior
> could be accounted for only by an assumption that he had
> no expectation of being alive much beyond Thursday. . . .
> Once this assumption was accepted, Hammett's way of life
> made a form of sense.[41]

And Sam Spade says to Effie Perine, "Somebody ought to write a book about people some time—they're peculiar."[42]

In 1978, Macdonald stopped seeing his psychiatrist, telling him that he thought his problems were now less psychological and merely "the encroachments of age."[43] The encroachments proved hard: Macdonald soon had symptoms of Alzheimer's disease and was diagnosed with it in 1981. Margaret had had lung cancer surgery in 1977 and now began to go blind from macular degeneration. "Here we are, two people who live by books," Margaret told a friend:

> What has happened has taken ninety percent of our lives away. I keep reminding myself of what we have left. I can't get out of it anyway. I've faced my own problems pretty well. I haven't faced his well, as least not as well as I think I should. . . . I lose my temper and then I go on guilt trips. The trips aren't as big as they used to be, but the temper remains the same.[44]

Margaret always said the truth as she saw it, and her words here speak to an eventual, tenuous contentment with each other, to which another of Margaret's friends attested:

> Margaret told me of one conversation where she sat down at his bedside and asked him, "Who am I?" and [Macdonald] looked at her and smiled and said, "The boss." Well, at once that's marvelously clever and marvelously sad. And marvelously true: she had taken his life over.[45]

Welty came to see him: "He looked at me and he said, 'I can't write.' And he looked at his hands."[46]

He was sixty-seven when he died in 1983. Lung cancer would kill Margaret at age seventy-eight in 1994. When Ross Macdonald was gone, his friend, English poet Donald Davie, said:

> I thought he was a brave man, very brave. I think he had a very curious and unhappy life. Born into an extraordinarily dislocated situation: Californian, lost his father, raised as a poor relation in Canada, then going to Michigan. . . . Nah, he'd started with most of the strikes against him. That he'd managed to put it all together and *get steadily better* for a long time—I thought it was wonderful.[47]

Conclusion

"You are what we want,"[1] *Black Mask* editor Joseph T. Shaw tells Hammett. Hammett, followed by Chandler and then Macdonald determinedly hammer their talents through to canons of unprecedented genre fiction.

Hammett invents the urban cowboy: the first lawman never to clean up the town, never make his mark, never get the girl, never have any money—never win. Hammett brings plausibility and realism to pulp fiction, mostly by making his detectives working-class wise guys of average smarts and unprepossessing physical prowess, who solve cases by getting all the suspects mad at each other and then seeing what happens. The Op cheerfully explains his strategy for closing the case in *The Dain Curse*: "I piled up what facts I had, put some guesses on them, and took a jump from the top of its heap into space."[2] In other words, in Hammett's fiction the figuring-out aspect of the plot is negligible.

Chandler poeticizes Hammett's prose and gives his hero true-feeling voice. "The things [the reader] really cared about, and that I cared about," Chandler says, "were the creation of emotion through dialogue [what he would also call 'the music'] and description."[3]

Chandler is concerned only about what the detective feels, so he isn't invested in plot at all. In 1946, William Faulkner is hired to write the screenplay for Chandler's *The Big Sleep*. He calls Chandler to ask who killed the chauffeur, and Chandler tells him he doesn't know.

As Macdonald puts it, "A close . . . relationship between writer and detective is a marked peculiarity of the form. Through its history, . . . the detective has represented his creator and carried his values into action in society."[4] Hammett borrows the hard-boiled detective from his own reports as a Pinkerton operative. He makes his first and most sustained character a fellow whose name is his function: the Continental Op. In Hammett's best novels, *Red Harvest* and *The Maltese Falcon*, the reader's attention is on what the detective does. Will the Op wind up "blood simple" in *Red Harvest*? Will Sam Spade turn in Brigid O'Shaughnessy?

The Op and Spade see working as intrinsically worthy and set rigid personal codes for themselves that protect their adherence to that ethic. If working is worthy and requires a code, and one under- cuts that code, then what? Being a detective provides an identity. In Hammett's novels, you are what your job is, which begs the question: What happens if you don't work?

The detective becomes a hero in Chandler's fiction, the sole para- gon of goodness in Los Angeles. "I'm a romantic," says Marlowe, "I hear voices crying in the night and I go to see what's the matter."[5] Chandler makes a knight-errant in a realistic novel, and Philip Durham explains the dynamic in *Down These Mean Streets a Man Must Go*:

> As a symbol the detective hero was superb, but as a symbol he could never achieve reality. The result was that Chandler was actually writing romantic fiction, by simulating reality through a hard-boiled attitude he could stay within an American literary tradition.[6]

For all that Chandler becomes the bard of American dislocation as fully realized in Los Angeles, Marlowe is implausibly and unrealistically untempted by all he comes upon as he restlessly roams. It makes him lonely; it means he has no one at all. "Let the phone ring, please," Marlowe says in an unguarded moment in *The Little Sister*.

> Let there be somebody to call up and plug me into the human race again. Even a cop. . . . Nobody has to like me. I just want to get off this frozen star.[7]

In the last sentences of Chandler's last letter, he mulled over Marlowe: "He is a lonely man. . . . I see him always in a lonely street, in lonely rooms."[8]

The murderers are hard-boiled women, and sex is always mixed up in it. In a Hammett novel, sex is fighting and winning; it is revenge and murder. "She was a beautiful fight-bred animal going to a fight," the Op says in "The Big Knock-Over."[9] The good woman is as dangerous to men as the bad. She may begin by adoring her man but, when he proves human and therefore sometimes in need of help, the veneration falls away, and she leaves him. A good one might soften an incautious man into weakness. In "Nightmare Town," Hammett writes: "He was afraid that if she tried to patch him up he would fall apart in her hands. He felt like that."[10] A good woman gives sex to get love. Hammett's stories and novels are frequently cautionary tales about what happens when women have the money, are in control, and are too close.

Marlowe plays Lancelot to female monsters, but he doesn't quite pull it off. He cannot be seen as a fully romantic hero, nor can Chandler. This is a key irony: Chandler is like his detective, yet neither man is what Chandler insisted on establishing. The dominant fault of his canon is the resulting hackneyed descriptions of

Marlowe's overheated attraction to sadistic women. As George P. Elliott describes it:

> The endless come-on to the certain cheat, that is the sort of women Marlowe dreamily desires. They arouse in him lust's nervous equivalent of infatuation. They are sex appellant and they do not promise love; yet it is never the pleasures of sensuality they want. They want to use him for some other end of their own.[11]

In psychoanalytic terms, Marlowe's showy interest in women is a reaction formation: exaggerated, affected, and counterfeit.

Genuine attraction and affection is between men. Would-be homosexual love is described by Chandler in inescapably wistful prose that creeps in through the edges of the battened-down hatches of Chandler's fiercely heterosexual stance. Marlowe is a tough and funny wise guy, but his loneliness is what soars—and it is sexual. Chandler makes Marlowe a man longing for other men, a cynic who believes in good and evil, and a lonely soul with a sense of humor: a man, in other words, very like himself.

Hammett may be afraid of his own attraction to women because it gives them control over him. Chandler is likely afraid of his desire for men, so he simulates an artificial interest in women. Both men stay away from what they want most.

The backstories of Hammett, Chandler, and Macdonald are testament to the impotence of the willed performance. A fair reading of Hammett is that anger, violence, and sex make him feel guilty as a child, that this same stew of urges are wed to his feelings about women when he becomes a man and make him guiltier still. He protects himself against these intolerable feelings by removing the triggers to his sources of shame—by having a code: no fighting, driving, or shooting. He keeps himself safely aloof from women and calls that stoicism. And he refuses monogamy, domesticity, and, eventually, sex. When he draws on his experiences as an operative to invent the hard-boiled genre, he also transfers his rules—personal-Pinkerton—to his detectives. Willy-nilly, the fundamental pull of repressed feelings undercuts Hammett's absolutist mindset and espoused forbearance. Alcohol and womanizing breach his self-control faster and worse. And, finally, in the long run of his detective-heroes, from pulp heroes to full-length novel protagonists, they derail their privileging of work and obedience to a code and are the authors of their own downfalls. And so the Op is beguiled by violence; Spade is seduced by Brigid O'Shaughnessy; and Nick Charles is a frantic alcoholic and self-conscious wit.

Dualities abound in Chandler's life: he is anxious in the company of women but stays in a long and hermetic marriage with a wife he loves and forgives. He is an unfaithful husband but after Cissy's death makes extravagant claims of fidelity and adoration. He is a nasty homophobe, but his English friends think he is a closeted homosexual. Chandler can't bear scrutiny, by himself or anyone else, so he creates an imaginary self and then lives as a recluse. When the loneliness hurts too much, he uses alcohol to effect an ersatz human connection, and then he drinks too much. Chandler's odd childhood sets him up for an odd adulthood in which he chronically misreads people in general and women in particular; in which being honest about himself to himself is so terrifying that he can't do it; and in which a writer of soaring prose for the disenfranchised urban little guy is himself sad, mad, drunk, and alone and cannot let himself think about why.

It is curious to think about Hammett's being able to stop drinking, while Chandler never stops or admits to the alcoholism that finally kills him. Only to himself does Hammett acknowledge his penchant for combinations of violence, anger, and sex and then manages the triggers. Chandler denies his desires, especially to himself. Apparently both men believe that their private feelings are so deserving of contempt that they cannot safely be shared. Neither man sets out to write self-realizing novels, and Chandler certainly sets out not to. In plain, Hammett and Chandler know without knowing; the evidence is there in their fiction.

M acdonald just knows:

> All men are guilty and all human actions are connected. The past is never past. The child is father to the man. And most of all, everyone gets what he deserves but no one deserves what he gets.[12]

Because Macdonald privileges connections between family members and repeating patterns between generations, he values plot over character and voice. "I see plot as a vehicle of meaning," Macdonald writes. "The surprise with which a detective novel concludes should set up tragic vibrations which run backward through the entire structure. Which means that the structure must be single, and *intended*."[13] The unlikely combination of genre detective fiction and psychoanalysis turns out to be apt: both start at a crisis point of suffering and work backward along chains of causality, looking at the ramifications of secrets.

Macdonald draws Archer as an acknowledger of universal fears. It is a complicated process because Macdonald writes himself into multiple characters and his own story into the connections between characters. "Certainly my narrator Archer is not the main object of my interest, nor the character with whose fate I am most concerned,"[14] Macdonald says.

> He is less a doer than a questioner, a consciousness in which the meanings of other lives emerge. This gradually developed conception of the detective hero as the mind of the novel is

not wholly new, but it is probably my main contribution to this special branch of fiction. Some such refinement of the conception of the detective hero was needed to bring this kind of novel closer to the purpose and range of the mainstream novel.[15]

Archer is almost as anonymous as a good therapist.

The murderer in Macdonald is frequently the angry mother of a son. She is killing to keep her son close, and there is a sexual feel to a motive grounded in perceived weakness. The mother Macdonald gets and the wife he chooses use weakness to keep him off balance and on the hook. His mother was psychologically fragile and given to hysteria. He can't rely on her. Macdonald's wife has a history of depression and suicidal thinking; throughout their marriage, he spares her the hardest parts of marriage and parenthood. He does not want his daughter to suffer her mother and grandmother's pain. In "Notes of a Son and Father," Macdonald begs for the power to "free her from fear and its false excitements, free her of the need to act out ever again an old heritage of trouble."

Macdonald's later novels turn on suffering children—usually sons—in fractured families and on what passes for love in those families, misshapen and usually between mothers and sons. Fathers in Macdonald's best novels fail to protect their sons by leaving them to mothers who then treat their sons like husbands. Macdonald's father does this: when he leaves his wife, he also leaves his son to her care, and she is unequal to the task—"without resources."

Macdonald is conflating the guilty-feeling, secret wounds of his childhood with psychoanalytic archetypes and the plots of classical myths to craft his fictional families. He is embracing what analysis and art have acknowledged for a long time: that poetry, painting, music, and fiction express overpowering yet repressed emotions. The feelings exposed are also personally meaningful to the viewer, the listener, and the reader. The conventions of the genre carrying the emotions—in Macdonald's case, hard-boiled detective fiction—provide a structure in which author and reader alike can safely wrestle dangerous feelings and a shared language that both parties understand. Unlike the anxious neurotic, the insightful participant in the author-reader conversation that is self-realizing fiction controls his fantasies. Moreover, the emotions in question are powerful because they are repressed; once they have been expressed, they are no longer determinative. So there is an informed, qualified optimism in Macdonald's work, carrying with it an indispensible feeling of membership in the wider world. "Tragedy happens when you lose what is most valuable to you," he says in an interview. "But that means you have *found out* what is valuable—and even have *had* it."[16]

Macdonald stretches Freud: mothers and fathers have Oedipal and Electra complexes too, says Macdonald, and they must not act on them. Mothers and fathers must relinquish their sons and daughters. In Macdonald's fiction, parents play at family romances too, conjuring perfect children. Parents must be mindful that these fantasy children—these Freudian vents—don't hurt their imperfect, actual daughters and sons. Oedipus and Electra complexes, family romances, folie à deux, repetition compulsion, conversion theory, and reaction formation: these are the psychoanalytic terms for the sufferings-in-common of us all, Macdonald shows in his last, best novels. And if the anxieties truly are universal, then it is always too late and never too late.

The Op, Spade, and Hammett believe that they can delineate right and wrong. Marlowe and Chandler think that they can judge what is good and evil. But Archer and Macdonald? They openly concede their own fallibilities. Each Macdonald character carries within him a capacity for, and a history of, right and wrong. As Archer says in *The Drowning Pool*, "Hers was one of those stories without villains or heroes. There was no one to admire, no one to blame. Everyone had done wrong for himself and others. Everyone had failed. Everyone had suffered."[17] Macdonald's is a forgiving worldview: let compassion and acceptance trump judgment and even personal responsibility. "My stories lack a powerful contrast between good and evil, because I don't see things that way," he says.[18] After his death, Welty writes, "What [Macdonald] was signaling to us in these fine and lasting novels is plain and undisguised: find the connections; recognize what they mean; thereby, in all charity, understand."[19] Forgiveness is always available in the simple recognition of one's shared humanity.

Notes

Introduction

1. Tom Nolan, *Ross Macdonald: A Biography* (New York: Scribner, 1999), 163–76.

2. Robert Gale, *A Ross Macdonald Companion* (Westport, CT: Greenwood, 2002), 210.

3. Ross Macdonald, "Notes of a Son and Father," Special Collections, University of California–Irvine Library, 1956, unnumbered.

4. Ibid.

5. Paul Nelson, "It's All One Case," in *Inward Journey: Reflections on Ross Macdonald by 25 of America's Most Distinguished Authors*, ed. Ralph B. Sipper (Santa Barbara, CA: Cordelia, 1984), 68.

6. Jerry Tutunjian, "Conversation with Ross Macdonald," in *Hard-boiled Mystery Writers: Raymond Chandler, Dashiell Hammett, Ross Macdonald: A Literary Reference*, ed. Matthew J. Bruccoli and Richard Layman (New York: Carroll & Graf, 1989), 295. Originally published in *Tamarack Review* 62 (1974): 66–85.

7. Ross Macdonald, "Down These Streets a Mean Man Must Go," *Anteus* 25–26 (Spring/Summer 1977): 211–16.

8. Diane Johnson, *Dashiell Hammett: A Life* (New York: Random House, 1983), 48.

9. Ross Macdonald, *Self-Portrait: Ceaselessly into the Past* (Santa Barbara, CA: Capra, 1981), 7.

10. Ross Macdonald, "The Writer as Detective Hero," in *The Mystery Writer's Art*, ed. Francis M. Nevins Jr. (Bowling Green, OH: Bowling Green University Popular Press, 1970), 301–302. Originally published in *Show* (January 1965): 34–36.

11. Macdonald, *Self-Portrait*, 27.

12. Ibid., 5.

13. Ibid., 37.

14. Leon Edel, *Literary Biography* (Bloomington, IN: Indiana University Press, 1959), 77.

15. Michael Kreyling, *The Novels of Ross Macdonald* (Columbia, SC: University of South Carolina Press, 2005), 86.

16. Edel, *Literary Biography*, 113.

17. "Ross Macdonald," 285.

18. Ibid., 90.

19. Edel, *Literary Biography*, 94–95.

20. "Ross Macdonald," 263.

21. Macdonald, *Self-Portrait*, 5.

22. Jerry Tutunjian, "A Conversation with Ross Macdonald," *Tamarack Review* 62 (1974): 66–85.

23. Nelson, "It's All One Case," 68.

Chapter One. Sons and Fathers

1. Edward Margolies, "Ross Macdonald: Gentle Tough Guy," *Which Way Did He Go?: The Private Eye in Dashiell Hammett, Raymond Chandler, Chester Himes, and Ross Macdonald* (New York: Holmes & Meier, 1982), 76.

2. Ross Macdonald, *The Doomsters* (New York: Alfred A. Knopf, 1958), 222.

3. Jerome Charyn, "Blue Eyes and the Barber King," *Inward Journey: Reflections on Ross Macdonald by 25 of America's Most Distinguished Authors*, ed. Ralph B. Sipper (Santa Barbara, CA: Cordelia Editions, 1984), 114.

4. Macdonald, *The Doomsters*, 240–41.

5. Ibid., 250.

6. Ibid., 238.

7. Ibid.,154.

8. Michael Kreyling, *The Novels of Ross Macdonald* (Columbia, SC: University of South Carolina Press, 2005), 95.

9. Ross Macdonald, *The Galton Case: A Lew Archer Novel* (New York: Warner Books, 1959), 194.

10. Ibid., 8–9.

11. Ibid.,195.

12. Ibid.,152.

13. Ross Macdonald, interview with Art Kaye, Kenneth and Margaret Millar Papers, University of California–Irvine Libraries' Special Collections and Archives, 31.

14. Ross Macdonald, *Self-Portrait: Ceaselessly into the Past* (Santa Barbara, CA: Capra Press, 1981), 61.

15. Macdonald, *Galton Case*,197.

16. Ibid.,196.

17. Ibid.,198.

18. Ibid.

19. Ross Macdonald, *The Chill* (New York: Bantam Books, 1983), 114.

20. Ibid.

21. Ibid.

22. Ross Macdonald, *The Blue Hammer* (New York: Alfred A. Knopf, 1976), 122–23.

23. Tom Nolan, *Ross Macdonald: A Biography* (New York: Scribner, 1999), 19; Macdonald, *Self-Portrait*, 5.

24. Ross Macdonald, interview with Paul Nelson, Kenneth and Margaret Millar Papers.

25. Macdonald, *Self-Portrait*, 12.

26. Ibid., 5–6.

27. Ross Macdonald, "Notes of a Son and Father," Special Collections, University of California–Irvine Library, 1956, unnumbered.

28. Ibid.

29. Macdonald, interview with Art Kaye, 34.

30. Macdonald, "Notes of a Son and Father."

31. Ibid.

32. Ibid.

33. Ibid.

34. Ibid.

35. Macdonald, *Self-Portrait*, 13.

36. Philip E. Slater, *The Glory of Hera: Greek Mythology and the Greek Family* (Boston: Beacon Press, 1968), 367–68.

37. Sigmund Freud, *Totem and Taboo*, standard edition (New York: W. W. Norton & Company, 1989), 161.

38. Sigmund Freud, *The Interpretation of Dreams* (New York: Avon Books, 1980), 296.

39. Michael Kahn, *Basic Freud: Psychoanalytic Thought for the 21st Century* (New York: Basic Books, 2002), 83.

40. Macdonald, interview with Art Kaye, 31–32.

41. Dashiell Hammett, *Five Complete Novels:* Red Harvest, The Dain Curse, The Maltese Falcon, The Glass Key, The Thin Man (New York: Avenel Books, 1980), 145.

42. George J. "Rhino" Thompson, *Hammett's Moral Vision* (San Francisco: Vince Emery Productions, 2007), 66.

43. Dashiell Hammett, "The Scorched Face," in *The Big Knockover: Selected Stories and Short Novels by Dashiell Hammett*, ed. Lillian Hellman (New York: Random House, 1966), 73.

44. William Marling, *Dashiell Hammett* (Boston: Twayne, 1983), 29.

45. LeRoy Lad Panek, *Reading Early Hammett: A Critical Study of the Fiction Prior to* The Maltese Falcon (Jefferson, NC: McFarland, 2004), 181.

46. Regina Combs Hammett, *History of St. Mary's County, Maryland* (Washington: Kirby Lithographic Company, 1977).

47. Joan Mellen, *Hellman and Hammett: The Legendary Passion of Lillian Hellman and Dashiell Hammett* (New York: HarperCollins, 1996), 20, 22.

48. Jo Hammett, *Dashiell Hammett: A Daughter Remembers*, ed. Richard Layman (New York: Carroll & Graf, 2001), 21.

49. Diane Johnson, *Dashiell Hammett: A Life* (New York: Random House, 1983), 23.

50. William F. Nolan, introduction, Dashiell Hammett, *Nightmare Town: Stories*, ed. Kirby McCauley, Martin H. Greenberg, and Ed Gorman (New York: Alfred A. Knopf, 1999), viii.

51. Johnson, *Dashiell Hammett*, 23.

52. Philip A. Kalisch and Beatrice J. Kalisch, *The Advance of American Nursing* (Boston: Little, Brown, 1978), 325.

53. Johnson, *Dashiell Hammett*, 23.

54. Hammett, *Red Harvest*, in *Five Complete Novels*, 134.

55. Ibid., 141.

56. Ibid.,102.

57. *Discovering The Maltese Falcon and Sam Spade*, ed. Richard Layman (San Francisco, CA: Vince Emery Productions, 2005), 69.

58. Dashiell Hammett, *Lost Stories*, ed. Vince Emery, intro. Joe Gores (San Francisco, CA: Vince Emery Productions, 2005), 86.

59. Johnson, *Dashiell Hammett*, 38.

60. Hammett, *A Daughter Remembers*, 32.

61. Frank Morn, *"The Eye That Never Sleeps": A History of the Pinkerton National Detective Agency* (Bloomington, IN: Indiana University Press, 1982), 151–52.

62. Sinda Gregory, *Private Investigations: The Novels of Dashiell Hammett* (Carbondale, IL: Southern Illinois University Press, 1985), 4.

63. Johnson, *Dashiell Hammett*, 65, 38.

64. Mellen, *Hellman and Hammett*, 26–27.

65. Dashiell Hammett, "From the Memoirs of a Private Detective," *Smart Set* 70 (March 1923): 88–90.

66. Joseph T. Shaw, unpublished draft of an introduction, Joseph T. Shaw Papers, 1936–1952, Department of Special Collections, University of California–Los Angeles Library, unnumbered.

67. Joseph T. Shaw, introduction, T*he Hard-Boiled Omnibus: Early Stories from Black Mask* (New York: Simon & Schuster, 1946), v.

68. Ibid., vi.

69. James M. Cain, *Double Indemnity,* in *Cain x 3* (New York: Alfred A. Knopf, 1969), 469.

70. Ed Sikov, *On Sunset Boulevard: The Life and Times of Billy Wilder* (New York: Hyperion, 1998), 197.

71. Ibid., 193.

72. Ibid., 204.

73. Raymond Chandler and Billy Wilder, *Double Indemnity*, in *Chandler: Later Novels and Other Writings* (New York: Library of America, 1995), 972.

74. Judith Freeman, *The Long Embrace: Raymond Chandler and the Woman He Loved* (New York: Pantheon Books, 2007), 218–19.

75. Sikov, *On Sunset Boulevard*, 198.

76. Tom Hiney, *Raymond Chandler: A Biography* (New York: Atlantic Monthly Press, 1997), 10.

77. Raymond Chandler, *The Long Goodbye* (London, UK: Penguin, 1959), 18.

78. Hiney, *Raymond Chandler*, 4.

79. Frank MacShane, *The Life of Raymond Chandler* (New York: E. P. Dutton, 1976), 6.

80. Eve Kosofsky Sedgwick, *Between Men: English Literature and Male Homosexual Desire*, in *Gender and Culture*, ed. Carolyn G. Heilbrun and Nancy K. Miller (New York: Columbia University Press, 1985), 23.

81. Raymond Chandler to Leroy Wright, March 31, 1957, in Jerry Speir, *Raymond Chandler* (New York: Frederick Ungar, 1981).

82. MacShane, *Life of Raymond Chandler*, 8.

83. Hiney, *Raymond Chandler*, 11.

84. Chandler, *Chandler: Later Novels*, 1055.

85. Raymond Chandler to Helga Greene, November 13, 1956, in *Selected Letters of Raymond Chandler*, ed. Frank MacShane (New York: Columbia University Press, 1981), 407.

86. Raymond Chandler to Hamish Hamilton, December 11, 1950, ibid., 250.

87. MacShane, *Life of Raymond Chandler*, 15.

88. Ibid., 22.

89. Ibid., 16.

90. Raymond Chandler to Hamish Hamilton, January 22, 1955, in *Selected Letters of Raymond Chandler*, 380.

91. Raymond Chandler to Hamish Hamilton, October 11, 1950, ibid., 236.

92. Raymond Chandler to Charles Morton, January 15, 1945, ibid., 46.

93. Ibid., 26.

94. Ibid., 32.

Chapter Two. Sons and Mothers

1. Michael Kreyling, *The Novels of Ross Macdonald* (Columbia, SC: University of South Carolina Press, 2005), 15.

2. Ibid., 86.

3. Ross Macdonald, *The Underground Man* (New York: Bantam Books, 1974), 147.

4. Ibid., 244.

5. Ibid.

6. Ibid., 47.

7. Ibid., 155.

8. Ross Macdonald, *The Chill* (New York: Bantam Books, 1983), 214–15.

9. Ibid., 46.

10. Ibid., 215.

11. Matthew J. Bruccoli, *Ross Macdonald* (San Diego, CA: Harcourt Brace Jovanovich, 1984), 39.

12. Macdonald, *The Chill*, 214.

13. Ibid., 215.

14. Ross Macdonald, *The Barbarous Coast* (New York: Alfred A. Knopf, 1956), 224–25.

15. John Utley, interview with author, June 29, 2009.

16. Macdonald, *The Chill*, 215.

17. Ibid., 211.

18. Ibid., 90–91.

19. Ibid., 114.

20. Ibid., 93.

21. Ibid., 193.

22. Arnold A. Rogow, *The Psychiatrists* (New York: G. P. Putnam's Sons, 1970), 241.

23. Macdonald, *The Chill*, 192.

24. Ibid., 215.

25. M. H. Abrams, "Psychological and Psychoanalytic Criticism," *A Glossary of Literary Terms* (Boston, MA: Thomson Wadsworth, 2005), 257.

26. Macdonald, "Notes of a Son and Father."

27. Ibid.

28. Ibid.

29. Ibid.

30. Ibid.

31. Ibid.

32. Ross Macdonald, *The Far Side of the Dollar, Ross Macdonald Selects Great Stories of Suspense*, intro. Ross Macdonald (New York: Alfred A. Knopf, 1974), 788.

33. Ross Macdonald, *The Instant Enemy* (New York: Alfred A. Knopf, 1968), 394–95.

34. Michael Kahn, *Basic Freud: Psychoanalytic Thought for the 21st Century* (New York: Basic Books, 2002), 108.

35. Macdonald, interview with Art Kaye, 1970, Kenneth and Margaret Millar Papers, University of California–Irvine Libraries' Special Collections and Archives, 36.

36. Tom Nolan, *Ross Macdonald: A Biography* (New York: Scribner, 1999), 20.

37. Ross Macdonald, "A Preface to *The Galton Case*, Afterwords," in *Hardboiled Mystery Writers: Raymond Chandler, Dashiell Hammett, Ross Macdonald: A Literary Reference*, ed. Matthew J. Bruccoli and Richard Layman (New York: Carroll & Graf, 1989), 263.

38. Nolan, *Ross Macdonald*, 23.

39. Ross Macdonald, "Notes of a Son and Father," Special Collections, University of California–Irvine Library, 1956, unnumbered.

40. Macdonald, *The Chill*, 198.

41. Phillip E. Slater, *The Glory of Hera: Greek Mythology and the Greek Family* (Boston: Beacon Press, 1968), 460.

42. Ibid., 461.

43. Macdonald, interview with Art Kaye, 34.

44. Ross Macdonald, *The Underground Man* (New York: Bantam Books, 1974), 224.

45. Macdonald, "Preface to *The Galton Case*," in *Hardboiled Mystery Writers*, 263.

46. Kreyling, *Novels of Ross Macdonald*, 86.

47. Nolan, *Ross Macdonald*, 34.

48. Macdonald, *The Chill*, 35.

49. Macdonald, "Notes of a Son and Father."

50. Ibid.

51. Terrence Real, *I Don't Want to Talk About It: Overcoming the Secret Legacy of Male Depression* (New York: Simon & Schuster, 1998), 143–44.

52. Eudora Welty, "Finding the Connections," in *Inward Journey: Reflections on Ross Macdonald by 25 of America's Most Distinguished Authors*, ed. Ralph B. Sipper (Santa Barbara, CA: Cordelia Editions, 1984), 155, 158.

53. Ross Macdonald, *Self-Portrait: Ceaselessly into the Past* (Santa Barbara, CA: Capra Press, 1981), 121.

54. Dashiell Hammett, *The Thin Man* (New York: Alfred A. Knopf, 1933), 129–30.

55. Ibid., 133.

56. Julian Symons, *Dashiell Hammett* (San Diego, CA: Harcourt Brace Jovanovich, 1985), 102.

57. Ibid.

58. Hammett, *The Thin Man*, 133.

59. Joan Mellen, *Hellman and Hammett: The Legendary Passion of Lillian Hellman and Dashiell Hammett* (New York: HarperCollins, 1996), 22.

60. LeRoy Lad Panek, *Reading Early Hammett: A Critical Study of the Fiction Prior to* The Maltese Falcon (Jefferson, NC: McFarland, 2004), 194.

61. Ibid., 16.

62. Dashiell Hammett, "The Ruffian's Wife," in *Nightmare Town: Stories*, ed. Kirby McCauley, Martin H. Greenberg, and Ed Gorman; intro. William F. Nolan (New York: Alfred A. Knopf, 1999), 58.

63. Ibid., 65.

64. Dashiell Hammett, *Red Harvest*, in *Five Complete Novels*: Red Harvest, The Dain Curse, The Maltese Falcon, The Glass Key, The Thin Man (New York: Avenel Books, 1980), 123.

65. Jo Hammett, *Dashiell Hammett: A Daughter Remembers*, ed. Richard Layman (New York: Carroll & Graf, 2001), 20.

66. Diane Johnson, *Dashiell Hammett: A Life* (New York: Random House, 1983), 70.

67. Dashiell Hammett to Blanche Knopf, March 20, 1928, in *Selected Letters, 1921–1960*, ed. Richard Layman (Washington: Counterpoint, 2001), 46.

68. Johnson, *Dashiell Hammett*, 222.

69. Ibid., 253.

70. Richard Layman, *Shadow Man: The Life of Dashiell Hammett* (New York: Harcourt Brace Jovanovich, 1981), 223.

71. Johnson, *Dashiell Hammett*, 245.

72. Julie M. Rivett, interview with author, October 17, 2008.

73. Hammett, *A Daughter Remembers*, 93.

74. Ibid., 152–53.

75. Ibid., 112.

76. Stephen Knight, "'A Hard Cheerfulness': An Introduction to Raymond Chandler," in *American Crime Fiction: Studies in the Genre*, ed. Brian Docherty (New York: St. Martin's Press, 1988), 82–83.

77. Ibid., 84.

78. *Philip Marlowe's Guide to Life: A Compendium of Quotations by Raymond Chandler*, ed. Martin Asher (New York: Alfred A. Knopf, 2005), 12–13.

79. Richard Layman, "Out From Under Hammett's 'Black Mask,'" in *Inward Journey*, 141.

80. Knight, "'A Hard Cheerfulness,'" in *American Crime Fiction*, 84.

81. Raymond Chandler, *The High Window*, in *Four Philip Marlowe Novels*: The Big Sleep; Farewell, My Lovely; The High Window; The Lady in the Lake, intro. Lawrence Clark Powell (Stamford, CT: Longmeadow Press, 1964), 359.

82. Ibid., 514.

83. Ibid., 515.

84. Tom Hiney, *Raymond Chandler: A Biography* (New York: Atlantic Monthly Press, 1997), 26.

85. Judith Freeman, *The Long Embrace: Raymond Chandler and the Woman He Loved* (New York: Pantheon Books, 2007), 146.

86. Hiney, *Raymond Chandler*, 48.

87. Freeman, *The Long Embrace*, 28.

88. Raymond Chandler to Deidre Gartell, March 2, 1957, in *Selected Letters*, 423–24.

89. Ibid., July 25, 1957, 455.

90. Raymond Chandler, *The Long Goodbye* (New York: Random House, 1953), 274.

91. Freeman, *The Long Embrace*, 28.

92. Frank MacShane, *The Life of Raymond Chandler* (New York: E. P. Dutton, 1976), 33.

93. John D. Gartner, *In Search of Bill Clinton: A Psychological Biography* (New York: St. Martin's Press, 2008), 25.

94. Freeman, *The Long Embrace*, 197.

95. Jerry Speir, *Raymond Chandler* (New York: Frederick Ungar, 1981), 138.

Chapter Three. Sons and Lovers

1. Tom Nolan, *Ross Macdonald: A Biography* (New York: Scribner, 1999), 170.

2. Ibid., 300.

3. Ibid., 307.

4. Eudora Welty, review of *The Underground Man* by Ross Macdonald, *New York Times Book Review* (February 14, 1971): 1, 28–30.

5. Eudora Welty, "Finding the Connections," in *Inward Journey: Reflections on Ross Macdonald by 25 of America's Most Distinguished Authors*, ed. Ralph B. Sipper (Santa Barbara, CA: Cordelia Editions, 1984), 155.

6. Ross Macdonald, *The Underground Man* (New York: Bantam Books, 1974), 120.

7. Peter Wolfe, *Dreamers Who Live Their Dreams: The World of Ross Macdonald's Novels* (Bowling Green, OH: Bowling Green University Popular Press, 1976), 314.

8. Macdonald, *Underground Man*, 244–45.

9. Ibid., 223.

10. Ibid., 130.

11. Ross Macdonald, *The Galton Case: A Lew Archer Novel* (New York: Warner Books, 1959), 198.

12. Macdonald, *Underground Man*, 132.

13. Ibid., 209.

14. Ibid., 15.

15. Ibid., 86.

16. Ibid., 136.

17. Ibid., 249.

18. Ibid.

19. Michael Kreyling, *The Novels of Ross Macdonald* (Columbia, SC: University of South Carolina Press, 2005), 143.

20. Macdonald, *The Underground Man*, 13.

21. Ibid., 230.

22. Nolan, *Ross Macdonald*, 46.

23. Ross Macdonald, "Notes of a Son and Father."

24. Edward Margolies, *Which Way Did He Go?: The Private Eye in Dashiell Hammett, Raymond Chandler, Chester Himes, and Ross Macdonald* (New York: Holmes & Meier, 1982), 72.

25. Macdonald, "Notes of a Son and Father."

26. Ibid.

27. Nolan, *Ross Macdonald*, 46.

28. Ibid.

29. John D. Gartner, *In Search of Bill Clinton: A Psychological Biography* (New York: St. Martin's Press, 2008), 25.

30. Margaret Millar to Ross Macdonald, October 4, 1948, Kenneth and Margaret Millar Papers, University of California–Irvine Libraries.

31. Gartner, *In Search of Bill Clinton*, 25.

32. Nolan, *Ross Macdonald*, 49.

33. Ibid., 48.

34. Ibid., 50.

35. Macdonald, "Notes of a Son and Father."

36. Nolan, *Ross Macdonald*, 60.

37. Macdonald, "Notes of a Son and Father."

38. Ross Macdonald to Anthony Boucher, December 9, 1947, in Nolan, *Ross Macdonald*, 88.

39. *Winter Solstice* notebooks and typescripts, Kenneth and Margaret Millar Papers.

40. Kreyling, *Novels of Ross Macdonald*, 38.

41. Nolan, *Ross Macdonald*, 51.

42. Ross Macdonald to Margaret Millar, September 9, 1945, Kenneth and Margaret Millar papers.

43. Margaret Millar to Ross Macdonald, March 4, 1945, ibid.

44. Margaret Millar to Ross Macdonald, n.d., ibid. The date is most likely 1945, given that the couple was apart due to Macdonald's military service.

45. Ross Macdonald, interview with John Stirn, US Information Service, January 1972, Kenneth and Margaret Millar papers.

46. Margaret Millar, *The Couple Next Door: Collected Short Mysteries*, ed. Tom Nolan (Norfolk, VA: Crippen & Landru, 2004), 55.

47. Margaret Millar, *Beast in View* (New York: Random House, 1955), 168.

48. Nolan, *Ross Macdonald*, 59.

49. Suzanne Marrs, *Eudora Welty: A Biography* (Orlando, FL: Harcourt, 2005), *355*.

50. Nolan, *Ross Macdonald*, 340.

51. Marrs, *Eudora Welty*, 489.

52. Ross Macdonald, *The Doomsters* (New York: Alfred A. Knopf, 1958), 171.

53. Ross Macdonald, *The Blue Hammer* (New York: Alfred A. Knopf, 1976), 187.

54. Ross Macdonald to Gerald Walker, January 6, 1974, in Nolan, *Ross Macdonald*, 352–53.

55. Dashiell Hammett, *Red Harvest, in Five Complete Novels:* Red Harvest, The Dain Curse, The Maltese Falcon, The Glass Key, The Thin Man (New York: Avenel Books, 1980), 20.

56. Dashiell Hammett, *The Dain Curse* (New York: Random House, 1929), 57, 64.

57. Sinda Gregory, *Private Investigations: The Novels of Dashiell Hammett* (Carbondale, IL: Southern Illinois University Press, 1985), 72–77.

58. Peter Wolfe, *Beams Falling: The Art of Dashiell Hammett* (Bowling Green, OH: Bowling Green State University Popular Press, 1980), 40.

59. Dashiell Hammett, *The Big Knock-Over: Selected Stories and Short Novels by Dashiell Hammett*, ed. and intro. Lillian Hellman (New York: Random House, 1966), 282.

60. John G. Cawelti, *Adventure, Mystery, and Romance: Formula Stories as Art and Popular Culture* (New York: Random House, 1962), 149, 156.

61. William F. Nolan, *Hammett: A Life at the Edge* (New York: Congdon & Weed, 1983), 19.

62. Jo Hammett, *Dashiell Hammett: A Daughter Remembers*, ed. Richard Layman (New York: Carroll & Graf, 2001), 28.

63. Ibid., 30.

64. Nolan, *Hammett: A Life at the Edge*, 18.

65. Andrea Barrett, *The Air We Breathe* (New York: W. W. Norton, 2007), 296.

66. Sue Miller, *The World Below* (New York: Alfred A. Knopf, 2001), 111.

67. Nolan, *Hammett: A Life at the Edge*, 21.

68. Dashiell Hammett to Jose Dolan, May 8, 1921, in *Selected Letters of Dashiell Hammett, 1921–1960*, ed. Richard Layman with Julie M. Rivett (Washington: Counterpoint, 2001), 18–19.

69. Dashiell Hammett to Jose Dolan, March 4, 1921, ibid., 10.

70. Julie Marshll Rivett, interview with Karen Karydes, October 17, 2008.

71. Lillian Hellman, *Pentimento* (Boston: Little, Brown, 1973), 140.

72. Joan Mellen, *Hellman and Hammett: The Legendary Passion of Lillian Hellman and Dashiell Hammett* (New York: HarperCollins, 1996), 37.

73. Diane Johnson, *Dashiell Hammett: A Life* (New York: Random House, 1983), 170–71.

74. Judith Freeman, *The Long Embrace: Raymond Chandler and the Woman He Loved* (New York: Pantheon Books, 2007), 64.

75. Ibid., 100.

76. Frank MacShane, *The Life of Raymond Chandler* (New York: E. P. Dutton, 1976), 40.

77. Jerry Speir, *Raymond Chandler* (New York: Frederick Ungar, 1981), 98–99.

78. Clive James, "The Country Behind the Hill," in *The World of Raymond Chandler*, ed. Miriam Gross (New York: A & W, 1977), 116.

79. Raymond Chandler, *The Big Sleep*, in *Four Philip Marlowe Novels:* The Big Sleep; Farewell, My Lovely; The High Window; The Lady in the Lake, intro. Lawrence Clark Powell (Stamford, CT: Longmeadow Press, 1964), 4, 24–25, 247.

80. Chandler, *The Big Sleep*, ibid., 107.

81. Michael Gilbert, "Autumn in London," in *The World of Raymond Chandler*, 116.

82. Chandler, *Farewell, My Lovely, in Four Philip Marlowe Novels*, 218.

83. Ibid., 286.

84. Ibid., 285.

85. Ibid., 552.

86. Peter Wolfe, *Something More Than Night: The Case of Raymond Chandler* (Bowling Green, OH: Bowling Green State University Popular Press, 1976), 50–51.

87. Michael Mason, "Marlowe, Men, and Women," in *The World of Raymond Chandler*, 94.

88. Raymond Chandler, *The Long Goodbye* (New York: Random House, 1953), 213.

89. William F. Nolan, *Hammett: A Casebook* (Santa Barbara, CA: McNally and Loftin, 1969), 41.

90. Freeman, *Long Embrace*, 140.

91. Raymond Chandler, "I'll Be Waiting," in *Chandler: Stories and Early Novels* (New York: Library of America, 1995), 572.

92. Raymond Chandler, "Kashinmor the Elephant," in *The Long Embrace*, 192–93.

93. Chandler, *The Long Goodbye*, 329.

94. Tom Hiney, *Raymond Chandler: A Biography* (New York: Atlantic Monthly Press, 1997), 108.

95. Raymond Chandler, "Chandler on His Novels, Short Stories, and Philip Marlowe," *Raymond Chandler Speaking*, ed. Dorothy Gardiner and Kathrine Sorley Walker (Freeport, NY: Books for Libraries Press, 1962), 207–209.

96. David Wyatt, "Chandler, Marriage, and the Great Wrong Place," *The Fall into Eden: Landscape and Imagination in California* (Cambridge, UK: Cambridge University Press, 1986), 164.

Chapter Four. Sons and Ghosts

1. Thomas Maier, *Masters of Sex* (New York: Basic Books, 2009), 285, 282.

2. Edward Margolies, *Which Way Did He Go? The Private Eye in Dashiell Hammett, Raymond Chandler, Chester Himes, and Ross Macdonald* (New York: Holmes & Meier, 1982), 71–72.

3. Raymond Chandler, *The Raymond Chandler Papers: Selected Letters and Nonfiction, 1909–1959*, ed. Tom Hiney and Frank MacShane (New York: Atlantic Monthly Press, 2000), 226.

4. Michael Kahn, *Basic Freud: Psychoanalytic Thought for the 21ˢᵗ Century* (New York: Basic Books, 2002), 123.

5. Ramond Chandler, *Four Philip Marlowe Novels*: The Big Sleep; Farewell, My Lovely; The High Window; The Lady in the Lake, foreword by Lawrence Clark Powell (Stamford, CT: Longmeadow Press, 1964), 319.

6. Chandler, *The Lady in the Lake*, ibid., 533.

7. Donald Spoto, *The Dark Side of Genius: The Life of Alfred Hitchcock* (Boston, MA: Little, Brown, 1983), 321.

8. Patricia Highsmith, *Strangers on a Train* (New York: Harper and Bros., 1950), 228.

9. Patrick McGillian, *Alfred Hitchcock: A Life in Darkness and Light* (New York: HarperCollins, 2003), 451.

10. Chandler to Bernice Baumgarten, May 14, 1942, in Raymond Chandler, *Selected Letters of Raymond Chandler*, ed. Frank MacShane (New York: Columbia University Press, 1981), 203.

11. Raymond Chandler, *The Long Goodbye*, in *Midnight Raymond Chandler* (Boston, MA: Houghton Mifflin, 1971), 587.

12. Ibid., 488–89.

13. Ibid., 733.

14. Raymond Chandler, introduction, *Trouble Is My Business* (Boston, MA: Houghton Mifflin, 1950), x.

15. Peter Wolfe, *Something More Than Night: The Case of Raymond Chandler* (Bowling Green, OH: Bowling Green State University Popular Press, 1985), 13.

16. Ibid., 51.

17. Chandler, *Farewell, My Lovely*, in *Four Philip Marlowe Novels*, 202.

18. Stephen Knight, "'A Hard Cheerfulness': An Introduction to Raymond Chandler," *American Crime Fiction: Studies in the Genre*, ed. Brian Docherty (New York: St. Martin's Press, 1988), 78.

19. Chandler to Jean De Leon, February 11, 1957, *Selected Letters of Raymond Chandler*, 421.

20. Chandler to Jessica Tyndale, August 20, 1956, ibid., 408.

21. Freeman, *Long Embrace*, 321.

22. Wolfe, *Something More Than Night*, 17.

23. John Houseman, "Lost Fortnight," in *The World of Raymond Chandler*, ed. Miriam Gross, intro. Patricia Highsmith (New York: A and W Publishers, 1977), 53–66. The quote is on p. 55. The essay originally was published in *Harper's Magazine*, August 1965.

24. Natasha Spender, "His Last Goodbye," in *World of Raymond Chandler*, 131.

25. Chandler to Jean De Leon, February 11, 1957, *Selected Letters of Raymond Chandler*, 421.

26. Freeman, *Long Embrace*, 172.

27. Chandler, letter to Leonard Russell, December 29, 1954, *Selected Letters of Raymond Chandler*, 374.

28. Dilys Powell, "Ray and Cissy," in *World of Raymond Chandler*, 86.

29. David Wyatt, "Chandler, Marriage, and the Great Wrong Place," in *The Fall into Eden: Landscape and Imagination in California* (Cambridge, UK: Cambridge University Press, 1986), 165.

30. Michael Kahn, *Basic Freud: Psychoanalytic Thought for the 21st Century* (New York: Basic Books, 2002), 81.

31. Ross Macdonald, "Notes of a Son and Father," Kenneth and Margaret Millar Papers, University of California–Irvine Libraries' Special Collections and Archives.

32. Ibid.

33. Tom Nolan, *Ross Macdonald: A Biography* (New York: Scribner, 1999), 177.

34. John M. Reilly, "Margaret Millar," *Ten Women of Mystery*, ed. Earl F. Bargainnier (Bowling Green, OH: Bowling Green State University Press, 1981), 239.

35. Margaret Millar, *Vanish in an Instant* (New York: Random House, 1952), 210.

36. Eudora Welty, review of *The Underground Man* by Ross Macdonald, *New York Times Book Review*, February 14, 1971, 1, 28–30.

37. George Grella, "Evil Plots," *New Republic* 173 (July 26, 1975): 24–26.

38. Paul Nelson, "It's All One Case," *Inward Journey: Reflections on Ross Macdonald by 25 of America's Most Distinguished Authors*, ed. Ralph B. Sipper (Santa Barbara, CA: Cordelia Editions, 1984), 67.

39. Ross Macdonald, *The Ferguson Affair* (New York: Alfred A. Knopf, 1960), 282.

40. Ibid., 177.

41. Ross Macdonald in "The Art of Murder" by Raymond Sokolov, *Newsweek*, March 22, 1971, 101–104, 108.

42. Ross Macdonald, *Sleeping Beauty* (New York: Alfred A. Knopf, 1973), 218.

43. Ibid., 28, 66.

44. Ibid., 66.

45. Ibid., 200.

46. Jo Hammett, *Dashiell Hammett: A Daughter Remembers*, ed. Richard Layman (New York: Carroll & Graf, 2001), 95–98.

47. Ibid.

48. Richard Layman, ed., foreword, *Selected Letters, 1921–1960* (Washington: Counterpoint, 2001), 7.

49. Hammett, *A Daughter Remembers*, 70.

50. Dashiell Hammett to Jo Hammett, May 24, 1944, *Selected Letters*, 332.

51. Hammett, *A Daughter Remembers*, 130.

52. Richard Layman and Julie M. Rivett, interview, "*The Maltese Falcon*: 75th Anniversary," washingtonpost.com, January 13, 2005.

53. Hammett, *A Daughter Remembers*, 79.

54. Ibid., 133.

55. Ibid.

56. Ibid., 134.

57. Doris Lessing, *The Sweetest Dream* (New York: HarperCollins, 2002), 68.

58. Julie M. Rivett, interview with Karen Karydes, October 17, 2008.

Chapter Five. After the Books

1. Susan Cheever, *Desire: Where Sex Meets Addiction* (New York: Simon & Schuster, 2008), 149.

2. Raymond Chandler, *The Little Sister*, in *The Midnight Raymond Chandler* (Boston, MA: Houghton Mifflin, 1971), 322.

3. Raymond Chandler, *Selected Letters of Raymond Chandler*, ed. Frank MacShane (New York: Columbia University Press, 1981), 405.

4. Cheever, *Desire*, 136, 139.

5. Chandler to Leonard Russell, December 29, 1954, *Selected Letters*, 373–74.

6. Chandler to Jessica Tyndale, October 21, 1955, ibid., 393.

7. Chandler to Tyndale, August 20, 1956, ibid., 409.

8. Chandler to Helga Greene, June 19, 1956, ibid., 402.

9. Chandler to Greene, February 11, 1957, ibid., 419.

10. Chandler to Greene, March 19, 1957, ibid., 429.

11. Raymond Chandler, *Playback* (Boston: Houghton Mifflin, 1958), 139.

12. John Tuska, *The Detective in Hollywood* (Garden City, NY: Doubleday, 1978), 302.

13. George V. Higgins, "Trouble in Mind," *Guardian Review*, June 17, 1988, 2.

14. Raymond Chandler, *The Long Goodbye*, in *Midnight Raymond Chandler*, 603.

15. William Wright, *Lillian Hellman: The Image, the Woman* (New York: Simon & Schuster, 1986), 70–71.

16. Jo Hammett, *Dashiell Hammett: A Daughter Remembers*, ed. Richard Layman (New York: Carroll & Graf, 2001), 108.

17. Dashiell Hammett, "Tulip," in *The Big Knockover: Selected Stories and Short Novels by Dashiell Hammett*, ed. Lillian Hellman (New York: Random House, 1966), 271.

18. George J. "Rhino" Thompson, *Hammett's Moral Vision* (San Francisco: Vince Emery Productions, 2007), 167.

19. Dashiell Hammett, "The Scorched Face," in *The Big Knockover*, 68.

20. John T. Irwin, *Unless the Threat of Death Is Behind Them: Hard-Boiled Fiction and Film Noir* (Baltimore: Johns Hopkins University Press, 2006), 198.

21. Dashiell Hammett, *The Thin Man*, in *Five Complete Novels:* Red Harvest, The Dain Curse, The Maltese Falcon, The Glass Key, The Thin Man (New York: Avenel Books, 1980), 726.

22. Diane Johnson, *Dashiell Hammett: A Life* (New York: Random House, 1983), 225.

23. Joan Mellen, *Hellman and Hammett: The Legendary Passion of Lillian Hellman and Dashiell Hammett* (New York: HarperCollins, 1996), 271.

24. Ibid., 259.

25. William F. Nolan, *Hammett: A Life at the Edge* (New York: Congdon & Weed, 1983), 190.

26. William Marling, *Dashiell Hammett* (Boston: Twayne, 1983), 119.

27. Lillian Hellman, *An Unfinished Woman* (Boston: Little, Brown, 1969), 239.

28. Hammett, *A Daughter Remembers*, 129.

29. Nolan, *Hammett: A Life at the Edge*, 199.

30. Ibid., 200.

31. Richard Layman, *Shadow Man: The Life of Dashiell Hammett* (New York: Harcourt Brace Jovanovich, 1981), 219–21.

32. Lillian Hellman, *Conversations with Lillian Hellman*, ed. Jackson R. Bryer (Jackson, MS: University Press of Mississippi, 1986), 67.

33. Dashiell Hammett, interview with James Cooper, "Lean Years for the Thin Man," *Washington Daily News*, March 11, 1957.

34. William F. Nolan, *Hammett: A Casebook* (Santa Barbara, CA: McNally and Loftin, 1969), 6.

35. Sinda Gregory, *Private Investigations: The Novels of Dashiell Hammett* (Carbondale, IL: Southern Illinois University Press, 1985), 180.

36. Steven Marcus, introduction to Dashiell Hammett, *The Continental Op* (New York: Random House, 1974), xvii–xxix.

37. Dashiell Hammett to Mary Hammett, February 12, 1941; Dashiell Hammett to Jo Hammett, June 30, 1949; Dashiell Hammett to Lillian Hellman, April 28, 1952—in Dashiell Hammett, *Selected Letters, 1921–1960*, ed. Richard Layman with Julie M. Rivett (Washington: Counterpoint, 2001), 168, 516, 584.

38. Hammett, *A Daughter Remembers*, 171.

39. Hellman, *An Unfinished Woman*, 225.

40. Marcus, introduction to *The Continental Op*, xv.

41. Nunnally Johnson, *Letters of Nunnally Johnson* (New York: Alfred A. Knopf, 1981), 187–88.

42. Dashiell Hammett, "Too Many Have Lived," in *Nightmare Town: Stories*, intro. William F. Nolan, ed. Kirby McCauley and Martin H. Gorman (New York: Alfred A. Knopf, 1999), 312.

43. Tom Nolan, *Ross Macdonald: A Biography* (New York: Scribner, 1999), 388.

44. Ibid., 404.

45. Ibid.

46. Ibid., 407.

47. Ibid., 415.

Conclusion

1. Diane Johnson, *Dashiell Hammett: A Life* (New York: Random House, 1983), 58.

2. William Marling, *Dashiell Hammett* (Boston: Twayne, 1983), 59.

3. Raymond Chandler, *Chandler: Later Novels and Other Writings* (New York: Literary Classics of the United States, 1995), 1034.

4. Ross Macdonald, "The Writer as Detective Hero," in *The Mystery Writer's Art*, ed. Francis M. Nevins Jr. (Bowling Green, OH: Bowling Green University Press, 1970), 295–96. Originally published in *Show* (January 1965): 34–36.

5. Raymond Chandler, *The Little Sister*, in *The Midnight Raymond Chandler* (Boston: Houghton Mifflin, 1971), 354.

6. Philip Durham, *Down These Mean Streets a Man Must Go* (Chapel Hill, NC: University of North Carolina Press, 1963), 96–97.

7. Chandler, *The Little Sister*, in *Midnight Raymond Chandler*, 354.

8. Raymond Chandler, *Selected Letters of Raymond Chandler*, ed. Frank MacShane (New York: Columbia University Press, 1981), 483.

9. Dashiell Hammett, "The Big Knock-Over," in *The Big Knock-over: Selected Stories and Short Novels*, ed. Lillian Hellman (New York: Random House, 1966), 316.

10. Dashiell Hammett, "Nightmare Town," in *Nightmare Town: Stories*, ed. Kirby McCauley, Martin H. Greenberg, and Ed Gorman; intro. William F. Nolan (New York: Alfred A. Knopf, 1999), 41.

11. George P. Elliott, "Country Full of Blondes," in *Hardboiled Mystery Writers: Raymond Chandler, Dashiell Hammett, Ross Macdonald: A Literary Reference*, ed. Matthew J. Bruccoli and Richard Layman (New York: Carroll & Graf, 1989), 69. Originally published in *Nation* 190 (September 4, 1960): 354–60.

12. George Grella, "Evil Plots," ibid., 308. Originally published in *The New Republic* 173 (July 26, 1975): 24–26.

13. Macdonald, "The Writer as Detective Hero," *Mystery Writer's Art*, 303.

14. Macdonald, "A Preface to *The Galton Case*," in *Hardboiled Mystery Writers*, 266.

15. Macdonald, "The Writer as Detective Hero," in *Mystery Writer's Art*, 304.

16. Peter Wolfe, *Dreamers Who Live Their Dreams: The World of Ross Macdonald's Novels* (Bowling Green, OH: Bowling Green University Popular Press, 1976), 242.

17. Ross Macdonald, *The Drowning Pool* (New York: Alfred A. Knopf, 1950), 230.

18. Ross Macdonald, "Farewell, Chandler," in *Inward Journey: Reflections on Ross Macdonald by 25 of America's Most Distinguished Authors*, ed. Ralph B. Sipper (Santa Barbara, CA: Cordelia Editions, 1984), 38.

19. Eudora Welty, "Finding the Connections," ibid., 158.

Bibliography

Abrams, M. H. "Psychological and Psychoanalytic Criticism." *A Glossary of Literary Terms*. 8th ed. Boston: Thomson Wadsworth, 2005. 256–62.

Anderson, Patrick. "American Style: Hammett, Cain, Chandler." *The Triumph of the Thriller: How Cops, Crooks, and Cannibals Captured Popular Fiction*. New York: Random House, 2007. 27–46.

Auster, Paul. *The Book of Illusions*. New York: Henry Holt, 2002.

Babener, Liahna K. "California Babylon: The World of American Detective Fiction." *Clues* 1, no. 2 (1980): 77–89.

Barrett, Andrea. *The Air We Breathe*. New York: W. W. Norton, 2007.

Bentley, Christopher. "Radical Anger: Dashiell Hammett's Continental Op." *American Crime Fiction: Studies in the Genre*. Edited by Brian Docherty. New York: St. Martin's, 1988. 54–70.

Bloom, Harold, ed. *Sigmund Freud. Modern Critical Views*. New York: Chelsea House, 1985.

Bridgman, Richard. *The Colloquial Style in America*. London, UK: Oxford University Press, 1968.

Bruccoli, Matthew J. and Richard Layman, eds. *Hardboiled Mystery Writers: Raymond Chandler, Dashiell Hammett, Ross Macdonald: A Literary Reference*. New York: Carroll & Graf, 1989.

———. *Kenneth Millar/Ross Macdonald: A Checklist*. Detroit: Gale Research/Bruccoli Clark, 1971.

————. *Ross Macdonald*. San Diego, CA: Harcourt Brace Jovanovich, 1984.

Budd, Elaine. "Margaret Millar: The Evil Within." *13 Mistresses of Murder*. New York: Ungar, 1986. 87–96.

Buntin, John. *L. A. Noir: The Struggle for the Soul of America's Most Seductive City*. New York: Harmony Books, 2009.

Cain, James M. *Double Indemnity*. In *Cain x 3*. Introduction by Tom Wolfe. New York: Alfred A. Knopf, 1969. 367–469.

Cawelti, John G. *Adventure, Mystery, and Romance: Formula Stories as Art and Popular Culture*. New York: Random House, 1962.

Chandler, Charlotte. *Nobody's Perfect: Billy Wilder, A Personal Biography*. New York: Simon & Schuster, 2002.

Chandler, Raymond. *Chandler: Later Novels and Other Writings*. Edited by Frank MacShane. New York: Library of America, 1995.

————. *Collected Stories*. Introduced by John Bayley. New York: Alfred A. Knopf, 2002.

————. *Four Philip Marlowe Novels*: The Big Sleep; Farewell, My Lovely; The High Window; The Lady in the Lake. Foreword by Lawrence Clark Powell. Stamford, CT: Longmeadow Press, 1964.

————. *The High Window*. New York: Random House, 1942.

————. *The Lady in the Lake*. New York: Alfred A. Knopf, 1943.

————. *Later Novels and Other Writings*. New York: Library of America, 1995.

————. *The Long Goodbye*. New York: Random House, 1953.

————. *The Long Goodbye*. London, UK: Penguin, 1959.

————. *The Long Goodbye*. New York: Random House, 1988.

————. *The Midnight Raymond Chandler*. Boston: Houghton Mifflin, 1971.

————. *Philip Marlowe's Guide to Life: A Compendium of Quotations by Raymond Chandler*. Edited by Martin Asher. New York: Alfred A. Knopf, 2005.

————. *Playback*. Boston: Houghton Mifflin, 1958.

————. *The Raymond Chandler Omnibus*. New York: Alfred A. Knopf, 1975.

————. *The Raymond Chandler Papers: Selected Letters and Nonfiction, 1909–1959*. Edited by Tom Hiney and Frank MacShane. New York: Atlantic Monthly Press, 2000.

————. *Raymond Chandler Speaking*. Edited by Dorothy Gardiner and Kathrine Sorley Walker. Freeport, NY: Books for Libraries Press, 1962.

————. "Requiem." January 1955. Department of Special Collections. University of California–Los Angeles Library.

————. *Selected Letters of Raymond Chandler*. Edited by Frank Mac-Shane. New York: Columbia University Press, 1981.

————. *The Simple Art of Murder*. New York: Random House, 1988.

————. *Chandler: Stories and Early Novels: Pulp Stories*; The Big Sleep; Farewell, My Lovely; The High Window. New York: Literary Classics of the United States, 1995.

————. *Trouble Is My Business*. Boston: Houghton Mifflin, 1950.

————. "Writers in Hollywood." *Atlantic Monthly* (November 1945): 116–25.

Cheever, Susan. *Desire: Where Sex Meets Addiction*. New York: Simon & Schuster, 2008.

Cline, Sally. *Dashiell Hammett: Man of Mystery*. New York: Arcade, 2014.

————. "Lillian Hellman and Dashiell Hammett: Treasures in the Archives." *Ransom Edition* (Fall 2007): 1.

Day, Gary. "Investigating the Investigator: Hammett's Continental Op." *American Crime Fiction: Studies in the Genre*. Edited by Brian Docherty. New York: St. Martin's Press, 1988. 39–53.

Dirda, Michael. "Dashiell Hammett (1894–1961): *The Maltese Falcon*; Other Works." *Classics for Pleasure*. Orlando, FL: Harcourt, 2007. 290–93.

Durham, Philip. "The *Black Mask* School." *Tough Guy Writers of the Thirties*. Edited by David Madden. Carbondale, IL: Southern Illinois University Press, 1968. 51–79.

————. *Down These Mean Streets a Man Must Go*. Chapel Hill, NC: University of North Carolina Press, 1963.

Edel, Leon. *Literary Biography*. Bloomington, IN: Indiana University Press, 1959.

Edenbaum, Robert I. "The Poetics of the Private Eye: The Novels of Dashiell Hammett." *Tough Guy Writers of the Thirties.* Edited by David Madden. Carbondale, IL: Southern Illinois University Press, 1979. 80–103.

Edmonds, Andy. *Frame-Up: The Untold Story of Roscoe "Fatty" Arbuckle.* New York: William, 1991.

Elliott, George P. "Country Full of Blondes." *Nation* 190 (September 1960): 354–60.

Ellis, David. *Literary Lives: Biography and the Search for Understanding.* New York: Routledge, 2000.

Engel, Jonathan. *American Therapy: The Rise of Psychotherapy in the United States.* New York: Gotham Books, 2008.

Freeman, Judith. *The Long Embrace: Raymond Chandler and the Woman He Loved.* New York: Pantheon Books, 2007.

Freud, Sigmund. "Family Romances." *The Standard Edition of the Complete Works of Sigmund Freud, 1906–1908.* Vol. IX: *Jensen's 'Gradiva' and Other Works.* 74–78.

———. *The Interpretation of Dreams.* New York: Avon Books, 1980.

———. *New Introductory Lectures on Psychoanalysis.* Edited and translated by James Trachey. New York: W. W. Norton, 1965.

———. *On Creativity and the Unconscious: The Psychology of Art, Literature, Love, and Religion.* Harper Perennial Modern Classics, 2009.

———. *An Outline of Psycho-Analysis.* Edited and translated by James Trachey. New York: W. W. Norton, 1949.

———. *The Problem of Anxiety.* Translated by Henry Alden Bunker. New York: Psychoanalytic Quarterly Press, 1936.

———. *Totem and Taboo: Resemblances Between the Mental Lives of Savages and Neurotics.* In *The Basic Writings of Sigmund Freud.* Translated and edited by A. A. Brill. New York: Modern Library, 1995. 773–898.

Gale, Robert. *A Ross Macdonald Companion.* Westport, CT: Greenwood Press, 2002.

Gartner, John D. *In Search of Bill Clinton: A Psychological Biography.* New York: St. Martin's Press, 2008.

Gay, Peter. *Freud: A Life for Our Time*. New York: W. W. Norton, 1988.

Gillam, Scott. *Sigmund Freud: Famous Neurologist*. Edina, MN: ABDO, 2012.

Goodstone, Tony, ed. *The Pulps: Fifty Years of American Pop Culture*. New York: Chelsea House, 1970.

Gores, Joe. *Hammett*. New York: G. P. Putnam's Sons, 1975.

———. *Spade and Archer: The Prequel to Dashiell Hammett's* The Maltese Falcon. New York: Alfred A. Knopf, 2009.

Gould, Warwick and Thomas F. Staley. *Writing the Lives of Writers*. Centre for English Studies, School of Advanced Study, University of London. New York: St. Martin's, 1998.

Grant, Robert and Joseph Katz. *The Great Trials of the Twenties: The Watershed Decade in America's Courtrooms*. Rockville Centre, NY: Sarpedon, 1998.

Gregory, Sinda. *Private Investigations: The Novels of Dashiell Hammett*. Carbondale, IL: Southern Illinois University Press, 1985.

Grella, George. "Evil Plots." *New Republic* 173 (July 26, 1975): 24–26.

———. "The Gangster Novel: The Urban Pastoral." *Tough Guy Writers of the Thirties*. Edited by David Madden. Carbondale, IL: Southern Illinois University Press, 1968. 186–98.

Gross, Miriam, ed. *The World of Raymond Chandler*. Introduction by Patricia Highsmith. New York: A & W, 1977.

Hall, Calvin S. *A Primer of Freudian Psychology*. New York: New American Library, 1954.

Hammett, Dashiell. *The Big Knock-Over: Selected Stories and Short Novels by Dashiell Hammett*. Edited and introduced by Lillian Hellman. New York: Random House, 1966.

———. *The Continental Op*. Edited and introduced by Steven Marcus. New York: Random House, 1974.

———. *Crime Stories and Other Writings*. New York: Library of America, 2001.

———. *The Dain Curse*. New York: Random House, 1929.

———. "Death and Company." 1930. *The Oxford Book of Detective Stories*. Edited by Patricia Craig. New York: Oxford University Press, 2000. 228–34.

————. *Five Complete Novels*: Red Harvest, The Dain Curse, The Maltese Falcon, The Glass Key, The Thin Man. New York: Avenel Books, 1980.

————. *Lost Stories*. Edited by Vince Emery. Introduction by Joe Gores. San Francisco, CA: Vince Emery, 2005.

————. "From the Memoirs of a Private Detective." *Smart Set* 70 (March 1923): 88–90.

————. *Nightmare Town: Stories*. Edited by Kirby McCauley, Martin H. Greenberg, and Ed Gorman. Introduced by William F. Nolan. New York: Alfred A. Knopf, 1999.

————. "Nightshade." *Vintage Hammett*. New York: Random House, 2005. 175–78.

————. *The Thin Man*. New York: Alfred A. Knopf, 1933.

Hammett, Jo. *Dashiell Hammett: A Daughter Remembers*. Edited by Richard Layman. New York: Carroll & Graf, 2001.

Hammett, Regina Combs. *History of St. Mary's County, Maryland*. Washington: Kirby Lithographic, 1977.

Hartman, Geoffrey H. "Literature High and Low: The Case of the Mystery Writer." *The Geoffrey Hartman Reader*. Edited by Geoffrey Hartman and Daniel T. O'Hara. Bronx, NY: Fordham University Press, 2004. 164–79.

Hellman, Lillian. *Conversations with Lillian Hellman*. Edited by Jackson R. Bryer. Jackson, MS: University Press of Mississippi, 1986.

————. *Maybe*. Boston: Little, Brown, 1980.

————. *Pentimento*. Boston: Little, Brown, 1973.

————. *An Unfinished Woman*. Boston: Little, Brown, 1969.

Herron, Don. *The Dashiell Hammett Tour: A Guidebook*. San Francisco, CA: City Lights Books, 1991.

Higgins, George V. "Trouble in Mind." *Guardian Review* (June 17, 1988): 1–2.

Higham, Charles. *Murder in Hollywood: Solving a Silent Screen Mystery*. Madison, WI: University of Wisconsin Press, 2004.

Highsmith, Patricia. *Strangers on a Train*. New York: Harper & Bros., 1950.

Hiney, Tom. *Raymond Chandler: A Biography*. New York: Atlantic Monthly Press, 1997.

Hoffman, Frederick. *Freudianism and the Literary Mind*. Baton Rouge, LA: Louisiana State University Press, 1945.

Hoopes, Roy. *Cain: The Biography of James M. Cain*. New York: Holt, Rinehart and Winston, 1982.

Houseman, John. "Lost Fortnight." *The World of Raymond Chandler*. Edited by Miriam Gross. Introduction by Patricia Highsmith. New York: A & W, 1977. Originally published in *Harper's Magazine* (August 1965).

Hughes, Dorothy B. *Erle Stanley Gardner: The Case of the Real Perry Mason*. New York: William Morrow, 1978.

Humm, Peter. "Camera Eye/Private Eye." *American Crime Fiction: Studies in the Genre*. Edited by Brian Docherty. New York: St. Martin's Press, 1988. 23–38.

Irwin, John T. *Unless the Threat of Death Is Behind Them: Hard-Boiled Fiction and Film Noir*. Baltimore, MD: Johns Hopkins University Press, 2006.

Jay, Paul. *Being in the Text: Self-Representation from Wordsworth to Roland Barth*. Ithaca, NY: Cornell University Press, 1984.

Johnson, Denis. *Nobody Move: A Novel*. New York: Farrar, Straus and Giroux, 2009.

Johnson, Diane. *Dashiell Hammett: A Life*. New York: Random House, 1983.

Johnson, Nunnally. *Letters of Nunnally Johnson*. New York: Alfred A. Knopf, 1981.

Kahn, Michael. *Basic Freud: Psychoanalytic Thought for the 21st Century*. New York: Basic Books, 2002.

Kalisch, Philip A. and Beatrice J. Kalisch. *The Advance of American Nursing*. Boston: Little, Brown, 1978.

Kardiner, Abram. *War Stress and Neurotic Illness*. New York: Paul B. Hoeber, 1947.

Kenner, Hugh. *A Homemade World: The American Modernist Writers*. Baltimore, MD: Johns Hopkins University Press, 1989.

Knight, Stephen. "'A Hard Cheerfulness': An Introduction to Raymond Chandler." *American Crime Fiction: Studies in the Genre*. Edited by Brian Docherty. New York: St. Martin's, 1988. 71–87.

Kreyling, Michael. *The Novels of Ross Macdonald*. Columbia, SC: University of South Carolina Press, 2005.

Krutnik, Frank. *In a Lonely Street: Film Noir, Genre, Masculinity*. London, UK: Routledge, 1991.

Kurzman, Dan. *Disaster: The Great San Francisco Earthquake and Fire of 1906*. New York: HarperCollins, 2001.

Layman, Richard. *Discovering* The Maltese Falcon *and Sam Spade*. San Francisco, CA: Vince Emery, 2005.

———— and Julie M Rivett. "*The Maltese Falcon*: 75th Anniversary." January 13, 2005, washingtonpost.com.

———— and Julie M. Rivett. *Selected Letters, 1921–1960*. Washington: Counterpoint, 2001.

————. *Shadow Man: The Life of Dashiell Hammett*. New York: Harcourt Brace Jovanovich, 1981.

Legman, Gershon. *Love and Death: A Study in Censorship*. New York: Hacker Art Books, 1963.

Lessing, Doris. *The Sweetest Dream*. New York: HarperCollins, 2002.

Lid, R. W. "Philip Marlowe Speaking." *Kenyon Review* 31 (1969): 153–78.

Macdonald, Ross. *The Barbarous Coast*. New York: Alfred A. Knopf, 1956.

————. *Black Money*. New York: Alfred A. Knopf, 1966.

————. *The Blue Hammer*. New York: Alfred A. Knopf, 1976.

————. *The Chill*. New York: Bantam Books, 1983.

————. *The Doomsters*. New York: Alfred A. Knopf, 1958.

————. "Down These Streets a Mean Man Must Go." *Anteus* 25–26 (Spring/Summer 1977): 211–16.

————. *The Drowning Pool*. New York: Alfred A. Knopf, 1950.

————. *The Far Side of the Dollar. Ross Macdonald Selects Great Stories of Suspense*. Introduced by Ross Macdonald. New York: Alfred A. Knopf, 1974.

————. *The Ferguson Affair*. New York: Alfred A. Knopf, 1960.

————. *The Galton Case: A Lew Archer Novel*. New York: Warner Books, 1959.

————. *The Goodbye Look*. New York: Alfred A. Knopf, 1969.

———. "Homage to Dashiell Hammett." *Mystery Writer's Annual* (April 1964): 8.

———. *The Instant Enemy.* New York: Alfred A. Knopf, 1968.

———. Interview with Art Kaye, 1970. Kenneth and Margaret Millar Papers. University of California–Irvine Libraries' Special Collections and Archives.

———. Interview with Paul Nelson. Kenneth and Margaret Millar Papers. University of California–Irvine Libraries' Special Collections and Archives.

———. Interview with John Stirn, US Information Service. January 1972. Kenneth and Margaret Millar Papers. University of California–Irvine Libraries' Special Collections and Archives.

———. *The Ivory Grin.* New York: Alfred A. Knopf, 1947.

———. To Margaret Millar. September 9, 1945. Kenneth and Margaret Millar Papers. University of California–Irvine Libraries' Special Collections and Archives.

———. *The Moving Target.* New York: Alfred A. Knopf, 1949.

———. *The Name Is Archer.* New York: Bantam Books, 1955.

———. "Notes of a Son and Father." Kenneth and Margaret Millar Papers. University of California–Irvine Libraries' Special Collections and Archives.

———. *Self-Portrait: Ceaselessly into the Past.* Santa Barbara, CA: Capra Press, 1981.

———. *Sleeping Beauty.* New York: Alfred A. Knopf, 1973.

———. *The Way Some People Die.* New York: Alfred A. Knopf, 1951.

———. "The Writer as Detective Hero." *The Mystery Writer's Art.* Edited by Francis M. Nevins Jr. Bowling Green, OH: Bowling Green University Press, 1970. 295–96. Originally published in *Show* (January 1965).

———. "Writing the Galton Case." *On Crime Writing.* Santa Barbara, CA: Capra Press, 1973. 25–45.

———. *The Underground Man.* New York: Bantam Books, 1974.

———. *The Wycherly Woman.* New York: Alfred A. Knopf, 1961.

———. *The Zebra-Striped Hearse.* New York: Alfred A. Knopf, 1962.

———— and Eudora Welty. *The Faulkner Investigation: William Faulkner's* The Hound *by Ross Macdonald, William Faulkner's* Intruder in the Dust *by Eudora Welty.* Introduction by Ralph B. Sipper. Santa Barbara, CA: Cordelia Editions, 1985.

McGillian, Patrick. *Alfred Hitchcock: A Life in Darkness and Light.* New York: HarperCollins, 2003.

MacShane, Frank. *The Life of Raymond Chandler.* New York: E. P. Dutton, 1976.

Mahoney, Rosemary. *A Likely Story: One Summer with Lillian Hellman.* New York: Doubleday, 1998.

Maier, Thomas. *Masters of Sex.* New York: Basic Books, 2009.

Margolies, Edward. *Which Way Did He Go? The Private Eye in Dashiell Hammett, Raymond Chandler, Chester Himes, and Ross Macdonald.* New York: Holmes & Meier, 1982.

Marling, William. *Dashiell Hammett.* Boston: Twayne, 1983.

————. *Raymond Chandler.* Boston: G. K. Hall, 1986.

Marrs, Suzanne. *Eudora Welty: A Biography.* Orlando, FL: Harcourt, 2005.

Martinson, Deborah. *Lillian Helman: A Life with Foxes and Scoundrels.* New York: Perseus Books Group, 2005.

Mellen, Joan. *Hellman and Hammett: The Legendary Passion of Lillian Hellman and Dashiell Hammett.* New York: HarperCollins, 1996.

Millar, Kenneth. "The Inward Eye: A Revaluation of Coleridge's Psychological Criticism." Dissertation, University of Michigan, 1952.

————. *The Three Roads.* New York: Alfred A. Knopf, 1948.

Millar, Margaret. *Ask for Me Tomorrow.* New York: Random House, 1976.

————. *Beast in View.* New York: Random House, 1955.

————. *The Birds and the Beasts Were There.* New York: Random House, 1967.

————. *The Cannibal Heart.* New York: Random House, 1949.

————. *The Couple Next Door: Collected Short Mysteries.* Edited by Tom Nolan. Norfolk, VA: Crippen & Landrue, 2004.

————. *The Fiend.* New York: Random House, 1964.

————. *It's All in the Family.* New York: Random House, 1948.

————. "The People Across the Canyon." *A Modern Treasury of Great Detective Murder Mysteries.* Edited by Ed Gorman. New York: Carroll & Graf, 1994. 1–15.

————. *The Soft Talkers.* London, UK: Victor Gollancz, 1957.

————. To Ross Macdonald, March 4, 1945, October 4, 1948. Kenneth and Margaret Millar Papers. University of California–Irvine Libraries' Special Collections and Archives.

————. *Vanish in an Instant.* New York: Random House, 1952.

Miller, Sue. *The World Below.* New York: Alfred A. Knopf, 2001.

Morn, Frank. *"The Eye That Never Sleeps": A History of the Pinkerton National Detective Agency.* Bloomington, IN: Indiana University Press, 1982.

Murphy, Mary. *Mining Cultures: Men, Women, and Leisure in Butte, 1914–1941.* Urbana, IL: University of Illinois Press, 1997.

Navasky, Victor S. *Naming Names.* New York: Viking Press, 1980.

Nelson, Paul. "It's All One Case." *Everything Is an Afterthought: The Life and Writings of Paul Nelson,* Edited by Kevin Avery. Introduction by Nick Tosches. Seattle: Fantagraphics Books, 2011. 397–400.

Nevins, Francis M. Jr. *The Mystery Writer's Art.* Bowling Green, OH: Bowling Green State University Popular Press, 1970.

Nolan, Tom. *Ross Macdonald: A Biography.* New York: Scribner, 1999.

Nolan, William F. *The Black Mask Boys: Masters in the Hard-Boiled School of Detective Fiction.* New York: William Morrow, 1985.

————. *Dashiell Hammett: A Casebook.* Santa Barbara, CA: McNally & Loftin, 1969.

————. *Hammett: A Life at the Edge.* New York: Congdon & Weed, 1983.

————. *The Marble Orchard: A Novel Featuring the Black Mask Boys: Dashiell Hammett, Raymond Chandler, and Erle Stanley Gardner.* New York: St. Martin's, 1996.

————. *Sharks Never Sleep.* New York: St. Martin's Press, 1998.

Nyman, Jopi. *Men Alone: Masculinity, Individualism, and Hard-Boiled Fiction.* Amsterdam-Atlanta, GA: Editions Rodopi B. V., 1997.

Orrmont, Arthur. *Master Detective: Allan Pinkerton.* New York: Julian Messner, 1965.

Panek, LeRoy Lad. *Reading Early Hammett: A Critical Study of the Fiction Prior to* The Maltese Falcon. Jefferson, NC: McFarland, 2004.

Penzler, Otto, ed. *The Black Lizard Big Book of Pulps.* New York: Random House, 2007.

Plumley, Stanley. Interview. *Washington Post,* August 13, 2008.

Podhoretz, Norman. "Another Part of the Forest: Lillian Hellman." *Ex-Friends: Falling Out with Allen Ginsberg, Lionel and Diana Trilling, Lillian Hellman, Hannah Arendt, and Norman Mailer.* San Francisco, CA: Encounter Books, 2000.

Poirier, Richard. *A World Elsewhere: The Place of Style in American Literature.* New York: Oxford University Press, 1966.

"Pulmonary Fibrosis." mayoclinic.com, accessed 2007.

Pynchon, Thomas. *Inherent Vice.* New York: Penguin Press, 2009.

Real, Terrence. *I Don't Want to Talk About It: Overcoming the Secret Legacy of Male Depression.* New York: Simon & Schuster, 1998.

Reilly, John M. "Margaret Millar." *10 Women of Mystery.* Edited by Earl F. Bargainnier. Bowling Green, OH: Bowling Green State University Popular Press, 1981.

Rich, Adrienne. *Of Woman Born: Motherhood as Experience and Institution.* New York: W. W. Norton, 1976.

Rivett, Julie Marshall. "On Finding My Grandfather's Love Letters." counterpoints.net, accessed 2004.

———. Interview with Karen Karydes. October 17, 2008.

———. "On Samuel Spade and Samuel Dashiell Hammett: A Granddaughter's Perspective." *Clues: A Journal of Detection,* 23, no. 2 (winter 2005): 11–20.

Rogow, Arnold A. *The Psychiatrists.* New York: G. P. Putnam's Sons, 1970.

Rollyson, Carl. *Lillian Hellman: Her Legend and Her Legacy.* New York: St. Martin's Press, 1988.

Rothman, Sheila M. *Living in the Shadow of Death: Tuberculosis and the Social Experience of Illness in American History.* New York: HarperCollins, 1994.

Ruhm, Herbert. "Raymond Chandler: From Bloomsbury to the Jungle—and Beyond." *Tough Guy Writers of the Thirties.* Carbondale, IL: Southern Illinois University Press, 1979. 171–85.

Samuel, Lawrence R. *Shrink: A Cultural History of Psychoanalysis in America*. Lincoln, NE: University of Nebraska Press, 2013.

Sarnecky, Mary T. *A History of the U.S. Army Nurse Corps*. Philadelphia, PA: University of Pennsylvania Press, 1999.

Schave, Richard and Kim Cooper. Interview with Karen Karydes. October 18, 2008.

Schickel, Richard. "Raymond Chandler, Private Eye." *Commentary* 35 (February 1963): 158–61.

Schopen, Bernard A. *Ross Macdonald*. Edited by Warren French. Twayne's United States Authors Series. Boston: G. K. Hall, 1990.

Sedgwick, Eve Kosofsky. *Between Men: English Literature and Male Homosexual Desire*. Edited by Carolyn G. Heilburn and Nancy K. Miller. *Gender and Culture*. New York: Columbia University Press, 1985.

Server, Lee. *Danger Is My Business: An Illustrated History of the Fabulous Pulp Magazines: 1896–1953*. San Francisco: Chronicle Books, 1993.

Shaw, Joseph T., ed. Introduction. *The Hard-Boiled Omnibus: Early Stories from Black Mask*. New York: Simon and Schuster, 1946. v–ix.

———. Joseph T. Shaw Papers, 1936–1952. Department of Special Collections. University of California–Los Angeles Library.

Sikov, Ed. *On Sunset Boulevard: The Life and Times of Billy Wilder*. New York: Hyperion, 1998.

Silvester, Christopher, ed. *The Grove Book of Hollywood*. New York: Grove Press, 1998.

Sipper, Ralph B., ed. *Inward Journey: Reflections on Ross Macdonald by 25 of America's Most Distinguished Authors*. Santa Barbara, CA: Cordelia Editions, 1984.

Slater, Philip E. *The Glory of Hera: Greek Mythology and the Greek Family*. Boston: Beacon Press, 1968.

"Smith Act." http://en.wikipedia.org/wiki/Smith_Act, accessed June 28, 2008. 1–5.

Sokolov, Raymond. "The Art of Murder." *Newsweek*, March 22, 1971, 101–104, 106, 108.

Speir, Jerry. *Raymond Chandler*. New York: Frederick Ungar, 1981.

Spoto, Donald. *The Dark Side of Genius: The Life of Alfred Hitchcock*. Boston: Little, Brown, 1983.

184   *Hard-Boiled Anxiety*

Stahl, Jerry. *I, Fatty: A Novel*. New York: Bloomsbury, 2004.

Stewart, Donald Ogden, ed. *Fighting Words*. New York: Harcourt, 1940.

Symons, Julian. *Dashiell Hammett*. San Diego, CA: Harcourt Brace Jovanovich, 1985.

Thompson, Bob. "An Ode to John Keats' Immortality." *Washington Post*, August 13, 2008, C1, C8.

Thompson, George J. "Rhino." *Hammett's Moral Vision*. San Francisco: Vince Emery, 2007.

Thompson, Josiah. *Gumshoe: Reflections in a Private Eye*. Boston: Little, Brown, 1988.

Trilling, Lionel. *The Liberal Imagination: Essays on Literature and Society*. New York: Viking Press, 1951.

Tuska, Jon. *The Detective in Hollywood*. Garden City, NY: Doubleday, 1978.

Tutunjian, Jerry. "A Conversation with Ross Macdonald." *Tamarack Review* 62 (1974): 66–85.

Utley, John. Interview with Karen Karydes. June 29, 2009.

Ward, Elizabeth and Alain Silver. *Raymond Chandler's Los Angeles*. Woodstock, NY: Overlook Press, 1987.

Weller, Sheila. *Dancing at Ciro's: A Family's Love, Loss, and Scandal on the Sunset Strip*. New York: St. Martin's, 2003.

Welty, Eudora. Review of *The Underground Man* by Ross Macdonald. *New York Times Book Review*, February 14, 1971, 1, 28–30.

West, Nathanael. *The Day of the Locust*. *The Complete Works of Nathanael West*. New York: Farrar, Straus and Cudahy, 1957.

Williams, Tom. *A Mysterious Something in the Night: Raymond Chandler, A Life*. London, UK: Aurum Press, 2012.

Wilson, Edmund. *The Boys in the Back Room: Notes on California Novelists*. San Francisco: Colt Press, 1941.

Wolfe, Peter. *Beams Falling: The Art of Dashiell Hammett*. Bowling Green, OH: Bowling Green University Popular Press, 1980.

———. *Dreamers Who Live Their Dreams: The World of Ross Macdonald's Novels*. Bowling Green, OH: Bowling Green University Popular Press, 1976.

————. *Something More Than Night: The Case of Raymond Chandler.* Bowling Green, OH: Bowling Green State University Popular Press, 1985.

Wright, Elizabeth. *Psychoanalytic Criticism: A Reappraisal.* New York: Routledge, 1998.

————. *Psychoanalytic Criticism: Theory in Practice.* New York: Methuen, 1984.

Wright, William. *Lillian Hellman: The Image, the Woman.* New York: Simon & Schuster, 1986.

Wyatt, David. "Chandler, Marriage, and 'the Great Wrong Place.'" *The Fall into Eden: Landscape and Imagination in California.* Cambridge, UK: Cambridge University Press, 1986. 158–73.

Index

A

Alexander, Muriel, 59
Aquinas, Saint Thomas, 81
Arbuckle, Fatty, 22
Archer, Lew, ix, xi, 1, 2, 3, 4, 7,
    8, 9, 14, 27, 38–39, 40, 41,
    42, 43, 45, 46, 48, 49, 53,
    70, 71, 72, 73, 74, 75, 80,
    83, 85, 97, 114, 115, 116
Arnstein, Nicky, 23
Auden, W. H., 82
Augustine, Saint, 81

B

Bachardy, Don, 109
Barbarous Coast, The, 41
Barrett, Andrea, 89
Beast in View, 83, 113
Beaumont, Ned, 86, 87, 132
"Big Knockover, The," 15

Big Sleep, The, 61, 96, 98, 100,
    107, 108
"Blackmailers Don't Shoot," 98
Black Mask magazine, 23, 25,
    26, 27, 87, 132
Blake, William, 81
"blood simple," 21
Blue Hammer, The, 9, 85
Brice, Fanny, 23
Bruccoli, Matthew, 41

C

Cain, James M., 27, 29, 30
Camus, Albert, 58
Cather, Willa, 58
Cawelti, John G., 88
Chandler, Cissy (Pascal), 35, 63–
    64, 66, 67, 93, 94, 95, 98–99,
    100–101, 110, 122–123, 124
    death of, 123

Chandler, Florence Dart
　　Thornton, 30, 31, 35, 63, 64,
　　66, 67, 93, 98
Chandler, Maurice Benjamin, 31,
　　32, 36
Chandler, Raymond, xi, xii, xiii,
　　xiv, xv, xvi, xvii, 2, 14, 15,
　　27, 28, 29, 30, 31, 32, 33,
　　34, 35, 36, 53, 60, 61, 62,
　　63, 64, 66, 70, 93, 94, 95,
　　96, 97, 98, 99, 100, 101,
　　103, 104, 105, 106, 107,
　　108, 109, 110, 111, 121,
　　122, 123, 124, 125, 126,
　　130
　　alcoholism of, 32, 94–95, 122,
　　　141
　　autobiographical fiction of,
　　　14–15
　　childhood of, 31–33
　　as confessional writer, xiv, 27
　　demise of, 123–26
　　detective of. *See* Marlowe,
　　　Philip
　　early career of, 33–35
　　education of, 32–33
　　identity issues of, 42–43, 109
　　infidelity of, 94, 141
　　influence of father on, 15,
　　　31–32
　　male authority figures of,
　　　33–34, 35–36
　　marriage of, 35, 93, 98–101,
　　　110, 122–23; first tipping

point of, 95; second tipping
　　point of, 100
　　role of Los Angeles in fiction
　　　of, x–xi, 61, 122
　　romanticism of, 34, 137–38
　　service in World War I of, 65
　　sexuality of, xiii, xiv, 103,
　　　104–105, 107–10, 140–41
　　women in fiction of, 66–67
Charles, Nick, 27, 55, 87, 128,
　　132
Cheever, Susan, 121, 123
Children's Hour, The, 129
Chill, The, x, 8, 36, 38, 40, 41,
　　42, 43, 46, 48, 51, 71, 74
Coleridge, Samuel Taylor, 80, 81
Continental Op, xi, 15–16,
　　20–22, 25, 26–27, 74, 83,
　　85, 86, 87, 91, 127, 128,
　　129, 132, 133, 150
Cooper, James, 131

D

Dain Curse, The, 2, 16, 25, 86, 87
Dante, 81
Darwin, Charles, 81
Davie, Donald, 136
De Beauvoir, Simone, 58
Descartes, René, 81
De Viane, Elise, 126
Devil Loves Me, The, 82
Doomsters, The, 1, 2, 3, 85
Double Indemnity, novel: 27; film
　　of, xiii, 28–30, 100

Drowning Pool, The, 145
Durham, Philip, 138

E

Edel, Leon, xiv, xvi
Elliott, George P., 140
Evans, Rose, 58–59

F

Farewell, My Lovely, 96, 105, 108
Far Side of the Dollar, The, 45
Faulkner, William, 138
Ferguson Affair, The, 114, 115
Fiend, The, 83
Fitzgerald, F. Scott, 128
"Fly Paper," 16
Ford, Bob, 77
Freeman, Judith, 63, 64, 67, 99
Freud, Anna, 134
Freud, Sigmund, x, xi, xv, 13, 32,
    36, 37, 41, 44, 45, 46, 54,
    55, 57, 58, 66, 67, 72, 77,
    81, 82, 93
  anxiety theory of, 46
  Civilization and Its Discontents,
    22
  Electra complex of, 111, 144
  family romances of, 44, 57, 63,
    67, 81, 144
  folie à deux (shared psychotic
    disorder), 28, 144
  Freudian psychoanalysis, 1,
    13, 14, 52, 81, 101, 111,
    124, 133

  inversion theory of, 104, 144
  Oedipal complex of, 9, 13, 36,
    43, 48, 77, 144
  phallic mother theory of, 54, 55
  repetition compulsion theory
    of, 66, 77, 92, 93, 101, 144
  Totem and Taboo, 13, 111

G

Galton Case, The, x, 4, 6–8, 14,
    36, 38, 49, 72, 74
Gartner, John D., 66, 77–78, 79
Gide, André, 58
Gilbert, Michael, 96
Glass Key, The, 86, 87
Granger, Farley, 106
Greene, Graham, 80
Greene, Helga, 33, 125–26
Gregory, Sinda, 24, 86, 132
Grella, George, 114
Guinness, H. S. H., 126
Gunnarson, Bill, 115

H

Hammett, Anne (Dashiell), 16,
    17, 19, 55, 56, 57
  death of, 23
  tuberculosis of, 17
Hammett, Josephine (Dolan)
    ("Jose"), 22, 23, 24, 25, 54,
    56, 59, 60, 91, 92, 101, 117,
    119, 126, 129
  courtship of, by Dashiell
    Hammett, 89–90

Hammett, Josephine *(continued)*
early life of, 88–89
pregnancies of, 24, 88, 90
Hammett, Josephine ("Jo")
(Marshall), 25, 57, 59, 60,
89, 117, 118, 126, 134
Hammett, Mary, 24, 26, 90,
117, 118, 119, 126. *See*
Hammett, Dashiell: paternity
question regarding first
daughter of
Hammett, Regina Combs, 16
Hammett, Richard (father), 16,
17, 19, 23, 36, 57
careers of, 17, 55–56
style of, 17
Hammett, Richard (brother), 16,
17
Hammett, Samuel Dashiell, xi,
xii, xiii, xiv, xv, xvi, xvii, 2,
14, 15, 16, 17, 18, 20, 21,
22, 23, 24, 25, 26, 27, 36,
50, 53, 54, 55, 56, 57, 58,
59, 60, 61, 62, 63, 70, 85,
86, 87, 88, 89, 90, 91, 92,
93, 97, 101, 103, 104, 116,
117, 118, 119, 126, 127,
128, 129, 130, 131, 132,
133, 134, 137, 138, 139,
140, 141, 142, 144
alcoholism of, 126, 127, 129,
134
autobiographical fiction of,
14–15
childhood of, 20–23
code in personal conduct of,
xii, xiii, 22, 24, 26, 140
communism of, 92, 129, 130
death of, 134
detectives of, xiii, xiv, 27, 53,
97, 132. *See* Beaumont, Ned;
Charles, Nick; Continental
Op; Spade, Sam
divorce of, 117
early career of, 18–19
education of, 18
father figures (fictional) of,
15–16; father figures (actual)
of, 23, 24
guilt as influence on, 20, 22,
26
influence of father on, 15,
17
on injuring others, 19, 20, 22,
88
marriage of, iv, 29, 91–92
military service of, 19,
129–130
paternity question regarding
first daughter of, xii, 90
as Pinkerton detective, xi, xii,
18, 19, 20, 22, 23, 25, 26,
130, 138, 141
prison term of, 23, 59–60, 130,
131
relationship with daughters,
xii, 57, 117–19
rudeness of, xiv, 17, 127

Hammett, S. D. *(continued)*
    termination of writing career of,
        127, 129–31, 134
    tuberculosis of, xii, 19, 23, 91,
        92, 134
    women in fiction of, 85–87,
        139
Hammettville, 16
Hard-boiled fiction
    "*Black Mask* School" of, 27
    the code, 27, 31
    conventions of, xi, xv, xvii, 4,
        14, 18, 22, 25–27, 131,
        144
    definition of, 62, 132
Hellman, Lillian, xii, 59, 90, 91,
        92, 101, 127, 129, 130, 131,
        134
    affair with Dashiell Hammett
        of, 92
    pregnancy of, 117
Hemingway, Ernest, 27
Higgins, George V., 126
Highsmith, Patricia, 105, 106,
        109
High Window, The, 62, 108
Himes, Chester, 104
Hiney, Tom, 30, 33, 64
Hitchcock, Alfred, 105, 106
Homosexuality, attitudes toward
    in the Hammett-Chandler
    era, 103
Horney, Karen, 82
Houseman, John, 109

I

Instant Enemy, The, 46
Invisible Worm, The, 82
"Inward Eye: A Revaluation of
    Coleridge's Psychological
    Criticism, The," 80, 81
Irwin, John, 128
Isherwood, Christopher, 110

J

James, Clive, 96
Johnson, Diane, 58
Johnson, Nunnally, 134
Jones, Ernest, xv
Jung, Carl, 82

K

Kahn, Michael, 13, 104, 111
"Kashinmor the Elephant,"
    99–100
Kierkegaard, Soren, 79
Kinsey, Alfred, 104
Klein, Richard, 32
Knight, Stephen, 61, 62, 108
Knopf, Alfred A., 55, 58, 84
Knopf, Blanche, 54, 58
Kreyling, Michael, xiv, 3, 49, 74,
        116

L

Lacan, Jacques, 32
Lady in the Lake, The, 94, 97,
        105, 108
Layman, Richard, 59, 61–62

Lessing, Doris, 119
"Lines with an Incense Burner,"
    65
Little Foxes, The, 129
Little, Frank, 22
Little Sister, The, 121, 139
Lloyd, Estelle, 35
Lloyd, Paul, 35
Lloyd, Warren, 34, 35, 36, 94, 98
Long Goodbye, The, xiii, 65, 97,
    100, 107

M

McCarthy, Joseph, 22
Macdonald, Ross, ix, x, xi, xii,
    xiii, xiv, xv, xvi, xvii, 1, 2, 3,
    4, 5, 6, 7, 8, 9, 10, 11, 12,
    13, 14, 15, 20, 22, 27, 36,
    37, 38, 41, 43, 44, 45, 46,
    47, 48, 49, 50, 51, 52, 53,
    63, 67, 68, 69, 70, 72, 74,
    75, 76, 77, 78, 79, 80, 81,
    82, 84, 85, 93, 101, 103,
    104, 111, 112, 113, 114,
    115, 116, 133, 135, 136,
    137, 138, 142, 143, 144,
    145
  autobiographical elements in
    fiction of, 2, 4–5, 6, 9, 14
  Canadian youth of, 1, 6–7, 10
  demise of, 135–36
  detectives of. *See* Archer, Lew;
    Gunnarson, Bill
  fairy tale, use of, 5–6
  on family guilt, x, 3, 6, 9, 10,
    11, 14, 47, 49, 51, 75, 116,
    143
  on fiction's ability to heal the
    writer, x, xvi, 6
  guilt: about daughter (Linda
    Millar), x, 51; about father
    (Jack Millar), 10, 12–13, 51;
    about mother (Anna Millar),
    51–52
  habit of stealing of, 10, 11
  health challenges of, 37
  impact of the past on, 6–7
  myth, use of, xv, xvii, 6, 12, 14,
    143
  psychoanalysis of, 1, 3, 13, 79,
    81, 101, 133, 135
  put up for adoption, 47
  reinvention of self, x, 1, 2, 12,
    51; reinvention of
    characters, 6
  as a son, 9–10
  sexual experience of: as
    adolescent, 10; homosexual
    encounters of, 11, 12, 50,
    82, 103, 104
  suicide attempt of, 103, 112
  women characters of, attitude
    toward sex, 1–2
McGilligan, Patrick, 106
MacMurry, Fred, 30
MacShane, Frank, 94
Maltese Falcon, The, 56, 86, 92,
    131, 132, 138

Marcus, Steven, 132, 134
Margolies, Edward, 104
Marling, William, 130
Marlowe, Philip, xii, xiii, xiv, 27, 61, 62, 63, 65, 67, 74, 83, 96, 97, 98, 99, 105, 107, 108, 125, 126, 138, 139, 140, 144
Marx, Karl, 81
"Mastermind, The," 81
Masters, William, 104
Maugham, Somerset, 123
"Memorial Day," 113
Mencken, H. L., 24
Millar, Anna ("Annie") (Moyer), x, 4, 6, 9, 38, 46, 47, 48, 49, 50, 51, 55, 75
  death of, 50–52, 75
Millar, Elizabeth, 10
Millar, Jack, x, 10, 11, 12, 47
  death of, 12, 50
Millar, Kenneth. *See* Macdonald, Ross
Millar, Linda, 1, 51, 82
  childhood of, 44–45, 79–80, 112–13
  death of, 69
  disappearance of, 37
  psychoanalysis of, x, 75
  vehicular homicide of, ix–x, 1, 45, 69, 112, 114
Millar, Margaret (Strum), x, 45, 69, 85, 101, 112–13, 135
  death of, 136

  early life and courtship of, 75–79
  writing career of, 81–83, 112
Millar, Rob, 10, 11, 12, 47
Miller, Sue, 89

N

Nathan, George Jean, 24
Nelson, Paul, xvii, 114
"Nightmare Town," 139
Nolan, Tom, 50, 77, 82
Nolan, William F., 88
"Notes of a Son and Father," ix, x, xii, 9, 44, 48, 51, 76, 78, 103, 112, 143

O

Oedipus, 5, 14, 32, 71, 80. *See* Freud, Sigmund: Oedipal themes

P

Pagnusat, James, 69–70, 75, 115
Panek, LeRoy Lad, 56
"Parthian Shot, The," 54, 55, 56
Pascal, Cissy. *See* Chandler, Cissy (Pascal)
Pascal, Gordon, 64
Pascal, Julian, 35, 64, 93, 94
Pearce, Donald, 83
Pentimento, 92
Perelman, S. J., 123
Pinkerton, Allen, 35
Playback, 125

"Poisonville," 58
Powell, Dilys, 110
Price, Reynolds, 84
Priestly, J. B., 123

R

Real, Terrence, 52
Red Harvest, xii, 15, 18, 20, 21,
     22, 57, 58, 85, 87, 131, 132,
     138
"Red Wind," 95
Rivett, Julie Marshall, 91, 119
Robinson, Edward G., 30
"Ruffian's Wife, The," 56
Ruhm, Herbert, 132
Russell, Leonard, 110

S

Samuels, Albert S., 24–25
"Scorched Face, The," 15, 128
"second city," xi, xvi
*Self-Portrait: Ceaselessly into the
     Past*, xi
Shaw, Joseph T., 23, 26, 27, 98,
     131, 137
Sikov, Ed, 29
Sipper, Ralph, 84–85
Slater, Philip E., 12–13, 48
Sleeping Beauty, 115, 116
Smart Set magazine, 24, 25, 54
Spade, Sam, xiii, 27, 74, 86, 91,
     97, 129, 132, 135, 138, 141,
     144
Speir, Jerry, 67

Spender, Natasha, 109, 124
Spender, Stephen, 109
Spoto, Donald, 106
Stanwyck, Barbara, 30
Strangers on a Train, xiii, 107
Symons, Julian, 55

T

Thin Man, The, xii, 54, 55, 87,
     127–28, 133
Thoreau, Henry David, 12
Thornton, Ernest, 31, 32, 33
Three Roads, The, 80, 81
"Trench Raid," 65
Trouble Is My Business, 107
Tuberculosis, attitudes toward,
     19
Tulip, 127
Tuska, Jon, 126
Tutunjian, Jerry, xvii, 74
Tyndale, Jessica, 123, 124

U

Underground Man, The, x, 8, 38,
     49, 70, 72, 74, 83, 114, 115

V

Van Vechten, Carl, 58
Vanish in an Instant, 113

W

Walker, Robert, 106
Watch on the Rhine, 127, 129
Weak-Eyed Bat, The, 82

Welty, Eudora, 135, 145
  affair with Ross Macdonald,
    83–85, 101
  "Finding the Connections,"
    52
  New York Times Book Review of
    The Underground Man, 70,
    114
Westlake, Donald, 127

Wilder, Billy, 27
  screenplay of *Double
    Indemnity*, 28–30
Winter Solstice, 80
Wolfe, Peter, 70, 71, 86–87, 97
Wright, Jimmy, 23
"Writer as Detective Hero, The,"
  xii
Wyatt, David, 100, 110

Acknowledgments

Professor David M. Wyatt, Department of English,
University of Maryland

Emeritus Professor Richard K. Cross, Department of English,
University of Maryland

Norman Colavincenzo, Literary Executor of the Estate of
Kenneth Millar and Trustee of the Margaret Millar
Charitable Trust; and Steve MacLeod and Audra Eagle Yun,
Special Collections and Archives, The UC Irvine Libraries,
Irvine, California

Tom Nolan, Author of *Ross Macdonald: A Biography* and
Coeditor of *Meanwhile There Are Letters: The Correspondence
of Eudora Welty and Ross Macdonald*

Julie Marshall Rivett, Granddaughter of Dashiell Hammett,
Author of "On Finding My Grandfather's Love Letters,"
Associate Editor of *Dashiell Hammett: A Daughter Remembers,*

Selected Letters of Dashiell Hammett, and *Return of the Thin Man, The Hunter and Other Stories*; Jo Hammett, Daughter of Dashiell Hammett, Author of *Dashiell Hammett: A Daughter Remembers*; and Richard Layman, Editor of the above titles, Dashiell Hammett Scholar, Biographer and Editor, Publisher and Editorial Director of Bruccoli Clark Layman Inc., and Director of Layman Poupard Publishing

Judith Freeman, Author of *The Long Embrace: Raymond Chandler and the Woman He Loved*

Amy Wong, Reference and Technology Services Coordinator, Library Special Collections, UCLA

Colin Harris, Superintendent, Special Collections Reading Rooms, Weston Library, Bodleian Libraries, University of Oxford, Oxford

Martha Lauzon, Library Associate, Special Collections & Archives, Dana Porter Library, University of Waterloo

Ron Sauder, Editor and Publisher, Secant Publishing

Susan Carini, Editor

The staff and patrons of the Talbot County Free Library

About the Author

Karen Huston Karydes had a twenty-four-year career at the Arlington County, Virginia, Department of Libraries, focusing on adult acquisitions and reference. She then ran the library for inmates inside the Arlington County Detention Center for five years. She has master's degrees in English from New York University and Library Science from the University of Maryland. At sixty, she pursued her interest in literary biography by entering the University of Maryland's PhD program in English language and literature. After receiving her degree in 2010, she returned to full-time public library work and is now the acquisitions librarian for the Talbot County Free Library in Maryland. She is also helping Edmund Wilson and William Faulkner scholar, Lewis Dabney, write a book about John Dos Passos. Her book, *Hard-Boiled Anxiety: The Freudian Desires of Dashiell Hammett, Raymond Chandler, Ross Macdonald, and Their Detectives*, is based on her dissertation.